MULTIPLE-PART BUSINESS FORMS
Their Function, Construction and Design

MULTIPLE-PART
BUSINESS FORMS
Their function,
construction and design

E. LENNOX MUIR

CASSELL · LONDON

CASSELL & COMPANY LTD
35 Red Lion Square,
London WC1R 4SJ

Sydney, Auckland
Toronto, Johannesburg

First published 1971

I.S.B.N. 0 304 93791 6

*To my dear wife Nancy for her great patience
as well as her valuable assistance; to the
late John MacLellan for his encouragement
and example; and to W. A. Thorne for
his kindness*

*Printed in Great Britain by
The Camelot Press Ltd,
London and Southampton*
F. 471

FOREWORD

It is obvious that the aim of this book is to offer assistance and guidance to those who have to originate multiple-part forms, whether this is an infrequent responsibility or a full-time occupation. It also quickly becomes apparent that there is plenty to interest both categories, regardless of the simplicity or complexity of their circumstances and equipment.

Above all, however, a common-sense attitude is maintained with regard to the simple explanations of every facet of each problem and solution, and the numerous diagrams are most helpful in clearly illustrating the points under discussion. Rather than provide a disjointed list of hints or suggestions, every encouragement is given throughout the text to stimulating cohesive individual thought, initiative, and imagination in order to overcome out-of-the-ordinary problems—and this can only be good for any business procedure.

The data-processing industry has little claim to any great antiquity, yet surely no industry has ever had such a volume of general and specific information written about it, and in such a brief period of time. All libraries offer an impressive selection of books and magazines on almost every conceivable aspect of this vast field—except, possibly, one area. That area is the end-product of the great majority of data-processing equipment, the multiple-part business form.

It is, therefore, opportune that an authoritative book on the subject has been written which will be published world-wide by a leading publishing company.

The author has shown an awareness of the necessity to develop and encourage a new mental attitude towards multiple-part business forms. This attitude demands a constant striving for maximum effectiveness in forms in all their aspects, the counterpoint being an intense and active dislike and intolerance of inefficiency in any procedure.

To this end the author obviously realized that the techniques and approach to paper-flow problems used by systems analysts could, and should, be more generally employed, even if to a much lesser degree than might be necessary in such as a computer installation. After all, the principles and purposes in designing a business form are exactly the same regardless of whether the writing instrument is the human hand, typewriter, accounting machine, or computer-output printer.

Clearly, the author has taken full advantage of his own considerable and comprehensive experience and training to write this unique and worthwhile text.

I wish good luck to this book, and every success to the reader.

DENNIS H. TRIGGS

Associate Director, Careers & Education Centre,
The National Cash Register Co. Ltd,
Greenford, Middlesex, England.

CONTENTS

LIST OF ILLUSTRATIONS

1 FUNCTION

'In the beginning . . . there were stock ruled sheets, and entries were made with a good quill pen.'

Whether pleased with the prospect or not, business administration is facing a situation similar to that which confronted industry following the turn of this century. At that time were spawned particularly the automotive giants who were certainly among the most successful in resolving problems relating to the then-new science of automated industrial production.

Their subsequent success was attained mainly because they were able to recognize at a very early stage in their development the basic necessity of reorganizing the mechanical complexities of their production departments with a high degree of efficiency. In the process a new mental approach to the problems of the work-shop had to be, and was, developed.

Of all the many generalities which appeared during this period of upheaval in thinking, surely one of the most significant remarks must be that attributed by many to Henry Ford. With apologies to the original author if imperfectly quoted, in effect the statement said, 'The tragedy about wasted time is that it does not pile up in great heaps on the floor.'

Few would now dispute that the largest single cost factor in any industry, whether manufacturing or service, is time. This is also the area in which the greatest waste is present—possibly just because it does not pile up in great heaps on the floor.

Conversely, of course, this is precisely the area in which the greatest savings can, and should, be made. Such savings in non-productive operations were one major economic feature which the early pioneers in the automotive field were so quick to recognize.

Their theories of efficiency in industrial techniques are now universally accepted without question, and have evolved into a real science. Their great wisdom, however, lay in their recognition that the proper utilization of time was the paramount factor in their mass-production techniques.

More important than the actual techniques was the development of a new mental approach to the problems of increasing efficiency. A new awareness of problems in organization and of the colossal cost and burden of inefficiency, plus an urgent enthusiasm, marked these men as admirable apostles of a new breed of clear-thinking administrators. They were, in fact, true professionals. Their power and prestige today indicates how well they learned and acted.

It is now being recognized, to a greater or lesser degree in various parts of the world, that business administration today is facing problems of inefficiency in the administrative field equal to, and possibly greater than, those which faced the pioneers in the industrial field. It also becomes more and more apparent in an industrial economy, although there are also many hopeful stirrings in the agricultural community, that a more advanced philosophy and mental approach must be acquired in relation to the over-riding importance of problems concerning wastage of time in administrative routines and procedures.

In case it is felt that the foregoing remarks apply only to large corporations, it should be clearly realized that tolerance of wastage of time will have as crippling and as stultifying an effect on a small company as it will on a larger company.

Just as the re-thinking on the factory floor was a direct result of the introduction of the new power equipment, so it is fair to recognize that the present crisis in administration has been largely generated by the advent of calculators, tabulators, computers, and other items of modern office equipment. However, it should equally be appreciated that manual routines are just as likely to warrant closer investigation.

It must be assumed that awareness of the need to install mechanical office equipment implies that, during the feasibility studies carried out before the actual installation, the necessity to alter procedures in the office has become apparent, and that at this time some more efficient procedures would already have been introduced because of the new equipment. But manual routines which have been in use for any lengthy period of time can, on inspection, often be found to be literally bulging with inefficiencies.

If at this point the reader feels some agreement with the foregoing, then the battle, while not yet won, can be claimed to have got off to a successful start.

As history will bear out, many battles have been won not necessarily by a preponderance of weapons and numerical superiority, but by a judicious choice of location, by common-sense assessments of the problems, and by a touch of imagination. In fact, by the correct mental approach—which is precisely the goal it is hoped the reader will attain.

The main purpose now is to consider how and where inefficiencies in administrative routines can be recognized, and to this end it may be that consideration should be given to what administration implies, and what part business forms play in the overall picture.

The Purpose of Administration

In general, business administration can be defined as the directing or superintending of the management of a business.

√Obviously, then, the effectiveness or otherwise of decisions relating to the efficient management of any business, large or small, will certainly be governed by the accuracy, reliability, and availability of information required by the administrators. On such information decisions will be formulated—always assuming, of course, that 'crystal ball' techniques have been discounted.

To digress for a moment, while there is no wish to become involved in spiritual matters of any sect or creed, it should be pointed out that decisions by 'divine guidance' are outwith the province of this text. It is felt that, in the long run, decisions based on factual evidence and data are on the whole more reliable than those made on 'hunches' or by inspiration. It sometimes seems that mere mortals have an aptitude for misinterpreting spiritual signs, and are on safer ground when applying their limited common sense to the more mundane facts in evidence before them. Providing, of course, that these 'facts' are really based on honest truth and known factors.

Reliable information must be readily available in order that effective decisions can be made by all levels of administration. It is, therefore, a proper and fair assumption to suppose that the more accurate, more detailed, and more current the relevant data are, the more quickly undesirable trends can be arrested or favourable policies noted, encouraged, plotted and controlled.

Decisions based on misapprehensions can hardly be expected to be effective, so in order that true assessments can be arrived at the data must be *accurate*. Furthermore, the more *detailed* the data the easier it will be to focus attention in depth to any specific area, and thus make effective critical comparisons. In the third place, it is important that the data should be *current* in order that developing trends can be quickly checked against historical data, and thereby provide a means for continuing control on a situation as it progresses.

The vital importance of the chain of communication through all levels in a business cannot be over-emphasized. If there is a breakdown or a bottleneck at any point in the pattern of administration, then the danger of an incorrect decision becomes increasingly probable.

Once such an adverse state of affairs becomes apparent it should not be tolerated for any length of time, and speedy action should immediately be instituted to remedy the offending routine.

All of this is obviously reasonable; but less obvious is the manner in which the problem should be tackled.

A point which is not always apparent is the need to understand that in any business there is a distinction between policy-making and administration, and yet there is a definite dependence of one on the other. If this dependence is not sufficiently well recognized, then a shrewd policy decision can be nullified by poor administration; while good administration, on its own, can at best only minimize the results of a bad policy decision. The one must support and complement the other.

Policy-makers must have an administration which will not only carry out the policy decided upon, but will implement it in such a manner that any adverse trends will become apparent and will be quickly brought to the attention of the appropriate authority for corrective action if this is felt to be necessary.

If, however, the chain of communication from the top to the bottom is not kept absolutely clear and free, then undesirable situations can develop and become chronic, while unfortunately remaining undetected until a major crisis arises. Or, perhaps even more dangerous, a situation allowing a slow but steady trickling away of potential efficiency may exist because, not having been accounted for in the first place, it may not be recognized at all. In times of close competition—and which times are not?—this can indeed be paralysing, if not fatal to the growth of a healthy company.

If the symptoms of these points of maladministration were obvious, then remedies would quickly be found. Like many medical maladies, however, the symptoms of industrial ailments are not always immediately apparent, and so diagnosis can be complicated unless we introduce means of making tests in our administrative structure—and then continuously enforce such tests.

However, it is equally important not to become a kind of industrial hypochondriac, and then to take the unfortunate step of over-prescribing measures to counter situations which may seldom or never arise. Then, unwittingly, the very weight of administrative paper-work routines may slow down every other routine or course of action.

Too often the cry arises in an industrious company that the 'weight of paper-work is smothering everything'—and too often the cry is well justified!

Parkinson's Law, however humorously conceived, is a greater factor in the administrative field, both in government bodies and in private companies, than most care to admit. A strong case exists for a parallel to Parkinson's Law which states 'Empty files tend to get filled up!' At a modest estimate it could be claimed that Mount Everest itself would be rivalled by clearing out the files of unrequired paper from any sizeable modern business community.

One of our main tasks, then, should be to find ways and means within our respective spheres to reduce such arrant waste of time and effort.

The Approach Preceding the Form

Too often a form's application either grows into an office routine without any real thought about its overall efficiency, simply because it does perform a particular function or fill a need, perhaps brought about by the introduction of a recent change in procedures. The criticism here is not that a change has been made, nor that something new has been added to the procedures. On the contrary, the proper attitude is to be aware that such changes will and should take place in any company that has a forward-looking and progressive policy. The offence is that such changes are made in a haphazard way, without due regard to other adjacent forms applications which might possibly be amended to provide the required information to the correct people or departments, thus avoiding duplication of effort all along the line and at the same time reducing the 'weight of paperwork'.

Inefficiency in such circumstances is invariably caused by a lack of coherent thought by management. It is the direct result of insufficient co-operation, wilful or otherwise, and it is not only a clear indication of a breakdown in the chain of communication but it also indicates the probability that this situation will in itself create further lapses of a similar nature.

A clear realization must be established that few, if any, forms applications stand on their own. On the contrary, most forms applications have a strong inter-dependence on other associated forms applications. It is too often apparent that the essential purpose of the information-storage function in a form design has been recognized—but that the equally important function of information-retrieval has been virtually overlooked. That is, it may be that the design of the source document is in no way conducive to a methodical and systematic procedure for the transference of the data from one document to another.

It is hoped that the foregoing observations may help to refute the impression that a form design is acceptable if it simply provides accommodation for necessary information. While this is the essential object, much more is required for a successful design than a pencil, a ruler, and a few spare moments.

Invariably, efficiency can only be attained by application of common sense, careful thought, and a detailed knowledge of the whole operation under consideration. Furthermore, it is at this stage that the great economies can be observed by all forms users whether large or small.

In this connection, management too often feels that it is making all the economy reasonably required if it is ensuring that the printed product is being bought at the cheapest price obtainable with the fastest possible delivery—without any regard to the functional ability of the form.

This attitude is really little short of criminal because, unlike most printed products, business forms are not finished when they leave the printer's factory; the truth is that their use is only now beginning. They are 'functional documents', and on their effectiveness of design and construction rests the question of whether or not the forms applications will be efficient and therefore economical.

A business form which is inefficient for one reason or another can induce further inefficiencies, the cost of which may be far greater than the total cost of the forms themselves. Beware, therefore, of buying inefficiency.

The True Cost of a Form

It is an interesting fact that the cost of business forms in themselves is by far the smallest cost factor in the overall total operating cost of a forms application. Yet when the word 'economy' is used the price of the forms is invariably the first point to be considered—and, unfortunately, is very often the only point which is considered.

As long ago as 1959 the United States National Archives and Records Service published their findings that for every unit spent in purchasing business forms *at least* 20 units were spent in handling, writing, using, distributing and filing these forms. Now, in view of the vast increase in the accumulated costs of labour—both in personnel expense and because of the advent of costly sophisticated data-processing equipment—it would be reasonable to assume that this disparity has increased by a further 50 per cent, to make handling costs at a conservative estimate 30 times the original cost of the forms.

For the sake of illustration, however, let us assume that the handling and processing expenses are still only 20 times the cost of the forms themselves. Even at that, it must still be apparent that the area begging for investigation with regard to economy should be the handling and procedure section rather than the actual cost of the form itself—although that should also be considered— since by improving efficiency in the form itself some procedural economies may be effected, even if this entails some additional cost.

The greatest possibilities for economy, however, must lie in increasing efficiency of procedures.

As can be seen, on the above basis a modest 10 per cent improvement in handling and processing far outweighs even an unrealistic 50 per cent saving in forms cost. To illustrate, let us assume the following:

'TOTAL COST' OF A BUSINESS FORM

Original cost	Units
Annual cost of business forms	1,000
Annual cost of handling and processing	20,000
	21,000 units

(1) *50% reduction in forms cost:*	Units	(2) *10% reduction in handling and processing:*	Units
Forms cost, less 50%	500	Forms cost	1,000
Handling, etc.	20,000	Handling, etc., less 10%	18,000
Total cost	20,500	Total cost	19,000
SAVINGS BY METHOD (1)	500	SAVINGS BY METHOD (2)	2,000

To even a casual observer, not only does this reduction in the annual procedural cost account for the *total* value of the forms for a *two-year period*, but it should not be overlooked that this 2,000-unit saving will apply virtually 'in perpetuity'. Furthermore, this is based on disparity figures which are now obviously out of date. Perhaps even a more easily obtainable 5 per cent reduction in the area of procedural costs would today achieve the same figure for savings.

It is hoped that the foregoing will emphasize the importance of starting our search for economy from the point at which the greatest degree of success is most likely. All approaches, of course, will be considered.

THE SURVEY

That an investigation into a forms procedure should be started is often quite obvious, but because of the complexity of our business structure it is more difficult for many to decide where, when, and how a forms application should be examined.

Why: It can be assumed that the examination of a forms application has become necessary for one or more of the following reasons:

(a) Because there has been a breakdown in control of a procedure;

(b) Because necessary information is not reaching the correct quarter quickly enough;

(c) Because an increase in the volume of work is overloading the structure;

(d) Because bottlenecks in procedure have become apparent through slowness of action in certain areas or in certain functions;

(e) Because an increase in the volume of statistics or analysed information is demanded in order to enhance company growth in an increasingly competitive market, while the effort to give such increased data could involve undesirable increased costs, unless new efficiencies can be made or existing inefficiencies can be eliminated;

(f) Because a business recession is forcing economies within the present structure;

(g) Because new, advanced office or manufacturing equipment is forcing a change in the present procedures;

(h) Or, more hopefully, because top management is conscious that in these days procedures should be regularly re-examined to ensure that inefficiencies will be eliminated, and that no new inefficiencies have crept in unnoticed since the last review. A wise management will anticipate such possibilities, and will not wait until one or other of the above potential catastrophes is imminent, because any remedies to such undesirable situations should not be taken on snap judgements but should be carefully examined to ensure that no new problems are inadvertently being created in the system.

All, or any, of the above circumstances can equally apply in any business, large or small.

Where to start: Experience will tend to substantiate that really the only place to start such an investigation is at the beginning of a procedure, rather than at the apparent point of dissatisfaction. The point of rupture or blockage of a procedure is actually the effect of the malfunction; the cause may well be at a considerably distant point.

A thorough investigation will have a triple benefit. Not only will all possibilities be properly explored and selected, but the efficient segments of the routine will be approved and will therefore be more confidently trusted; and, equally important, an opportunity will be afforded to either write-up or flow-chart each procedure in detail for future reference. By such means, it is a simple matter to check periodically that the eventual approved procedure is being correctly implemented.

Similarly, should a subsequent procedural change be anticipated or proposed, then all the relevant data will be readily available to make a quick and accurate evaluation of the effectiveness of such a proposed change.

Since, because of differences in personnel, equipment, plant, products and services, it is unlikely that any two businesses anywhere in the world will be exactly the same, it should be realized that there are no hard-and-fast rules that can be laid down for unqualified acceptance. On the contrary, the correct approach for any systems analysis must be that no practices, however highly respected or generally accepted, are beyond questioning. Routines which may have been correct and desirable two years ago, for instance, may now be quite unacceptable for present-day circumstances, and are certainly worth reappraisal. Conversely, simply because a procedure has been in use for a period of time, this does not mean that it unquestionably *must* be changed—it is only suggested that it should be looked at closely.

The whole point of these observations is simply that nothing must be taken for granted; everything related to a procedure must be examined closely at regular intervals.

Some mention at this point should also be made regarding the method of conducting even the most simple systems study—and study it should be. Let there be no confusion of our objectives. Our aim is to study the facts of a procedure—as they actually are—and not just the taking of a superficial look at an 'outline' of a procedure which may have been diligently written up, or even flow-charted, at the time of instituting that particular routine.

The procedure written up for a routine and the manner in which it is actually carried out are very often found to be vastly different in many ways—and sometimes the digressions are made for very valid and logical reasons. These reasons are frequently the bases for proposed changes. On the other hand, digressions from a laid-down procedure are also frequently the result of slackness and lack of supervision, or even a lack of understanding of the whole routine, and again this situation may be an indication that some change in the routine is desirable.

It is often not fully recognized that routine work can become unbearably boring because of lack of understanding, thus inducing indifference and inefficiency, unless the operatives concerned are properly instructed and impressed with the ultimate result of their labours. An interested and enthusiastic employee, regardless of how humble his position in the organization, is invariably much more efficient and effective than one who is bored and who feels that neither he nor his efforts are of any consequence. He must be, and feel, involved.

The correct mental attitude must be cultivated to any systems survey, even a very elementary 'walk-through' study, so that at all times a humane approach is applied to the problems in order to induce maximum response.

Machines can be mass-produced to precise tolerances, and can be programmed or directed to produce exactly to precise requirements. People, however, are different.

It is, therefore, of the utmost importance to decide who should personally conduct any serious study of a routine. That is, who should undertake the actual spade-work, the fact-finding enquiry.

Fact-Finding

The key figure will usually be the office or departmental manager, or someone with manager status. However, while it may be the direct responsibility of the manager to institute such a study, and in fact it will usually be decidedly to his advantage that such a study should be made, it is seldom that he is the correct person to undertake this project on his own, for a number of quite obvious, and some not so obvious, reasons.

Among such reasons are the following:

(1) Most managers have many urgent administrative duties which could preclude the possibility that time may have to be taken off to delve quite deeply into each facet of what could become a highly involved and time-consuming operation. Much time may also be spent in areas which will prove negative in the end.

(2) It would be extremely difficult, because a manager is so deeply involved with other problems, for him to approach the situation with the impartial mind which is so desirable for maximum benefit.

(3) Despite the possibility that he probably knows more than anyone else about how the routine should function, it should be recognized that this very fact that he is so totally conversant with the procedure may incline him to assume that functions are being performed in a certain manner because that is how they should be done, rather than to investigate how they are being done in practice. However, the manager's advice on whether or not a proposed change should be adopted must be eventually sought and acted upon. His *must* be the *final* word.

(4) The very seniority of the manager's position in relation to his subordinates, who perform the functions of any routine, may in many cases serve as a barrier to obtaining entirely honest answers to perhaps embarrassing questions. The tendency may be to give an answer which it is felt will be what is desirable, rather than that which is actual fact. After all, who amongst us is particularly anxious to calmly advise 'the boss' that we have not been carrying out instructions for some reason which might inspire a less-than-favourable reaction? The instinct is, to be charitable, an inclination to put up a diversionary smokescreen.

An approach from a less commanding and imposing person is usually more successful in eliciting little-advertised information.

Psychologically, there is a considerable art in obtaining such information which is well worth cultivating, and beneficial results are more likely if the person being questioned is not made to feel that his head is on the block and the chopper is about to fall.

Everything must be done to create an atmosphere of confidence. Not only should the operative be made to feel that his duties are of importance but that his assistance and advice is being sought—and will be given serious consideration. He must be made to feel that he is involved. Frequently, much good advice is obtained from just such sources, and logical reasons can be advanced for not adhering to a laid-down procedure. However, the possibility of recriminations and retribution will do little to encourage plain talking.

(5) In some cases a manager may have a misguided sense of loyalty to those who devised the present system. However high his motives may be in this matter, such protective instincts must be carefully controlled because it must be clearly understood that what is being conducted is an honest effort to improve efficiency in a way that will benefit everyone involved. There must not be the remotest possibility of the operation being misconstrued as a 'witch-hunt'.

(6) Finally, while it is of the utmost importance that the whole truth be known, the necessary information should be extracted with the minimum of disruption or disturbance. Therefore, when it is felt that full co-operation is not being obtained, in order to avoid a head-on confrontation and a possible breach in relations, it is easier for someone of less importance to back off and seek another approach than would be the case if the authority of the manager was thus put at stake.

From the foregoing it should not be misconstrued that the manager is of relatively little importance in this operation. On the contrary, he is by far the most important link in the chain. But his value lies in his knowledge and experience in controlling the survey, and in his ability to designate his authority to the proper people, and in finally providing the official stamp of approval by his acceptance of the eventual proposals. The 'digging' can often be entrusted to a subordinate—always assuming that someone of intelligence, tact, and common sense is appointed.

The final success of any system, however, is the direct responsibility of the manager.

Co-operation and Consultation

While much lip-service is paid to the principles of co-operation and consultation, too often these principles are not carried into practice. However, without co-operation and consultation there can be no co-ordination, and it must be obvious that no procedure can be remotely systematic without these three ingredients.

People are largely creatures of habit and so changes from normal routines, particularly if suddenly introduced without proper explanation, can evoke quite violent feelings of insecurity which, in turn, can produce damaging opposition to a new routine.

There is a school of thought which considers that routines are the exclusive right of administrators, and that no interference or criticism should be tolerated. The theory is that if a routine is laid down and insisted upon for long enough, then, in time, everything will settle down—and if it doesn't, then this is the result of 'saboteurs'.

Experience will conclusively show, however, that the loss of time and efficiency incurred by this method is invariably enormous. It will usually be found that the settling down does not take place until certain changes are made, involving further disruption.

These changes should have been made before the routine was laid down, thus avoiding hostility and acts of non-co-operation. Common sense should indicate that hostility and reluctance on the part of personnel implementing a procedure can play havoc with any routine, however well devised it may be.

An indication of a break-through into the correct mental attitude to modern-day administration is the ability to recognize this necessity for co-operation, before any effective degree of co-ordination can be reasonably expected in any procedure. It is profitable to recognize this from the very beginning.

How to Start a Survey

When the necessity for a systems study is proposed for one or more of the reasons previously mentioned, then the senior administrator involved, for example the office manager, should hold a meeting of those responsible for using and implementing the procedure. At this stage the arguments for and against a study should be carefully examined, and if it is decided that some improvement is feasible, then the main objectives should be clearly established and outlined.

Following this, and presuming that there is not already a Systems and

Procedures Department, someone should be appointed to carry out the fact-finding duties, with his responsibilities clearly indicated. A further brief meeting should be called, not only with those already consulted, but also with the heads of all departments who may be involved, even if only indirectly, and again the problems should be explained and the objectives outlined.

This latter meeting has a two-fold purpose. First, in order that everyone should be left in no doubt that the fact-finder has full authority to probe as deeply as he feels is necessary, and to confirm that he should be allowed free access to all sources of information—always, of course, with due regard to the responsibilities of the heads of each department. Second, and probably more important, every effort should be made to *convince* those present of the importance of their contribution to the study, particularly in the matter of their co-operation. It is important that they should feel that this is very much a team effort, and that their enthusiasm and co-operation is vital for success.

However, beware of the over-zealous who may wish to 'save time' by elaborating immediately on his department's contribution to a system. The interjection must be stopped. Opinions are not required at this stage. Each actual fact must be verified by the personnel performing the operation—and second-hand opinions, however conscientiously offered, must be ignored and the fact-finding done on the spot by the fact-finder.

It should be made very clear that this fact-finder is the only one, under the direct authority of the manager, who will ascertain the facts. Each person connected in any way with the procedure will, in turn, be contacted and information and advice will be sought. Everyone who feels that he or she has something to contribute will be heard—but only at the correct time in the programme.

This should be emphasized to forestall well-meaning approaches being made to the fact-finder until he is ready for that particular section. The fact-finder must not be diverted from approaching the problems in a systematic manner.

It must be realized, of course, that the foregoing remarks are intended for an organization which does not have a Systems and Procedures Department, but it will be agreed that the general approach would be the same if such a department did exist.

Nor should it be assumed that prior knowledge of the procedure under review is necessary or even desirable. While an experienced systems analyst would be of great assistance later, at this fact-finding stage at least as much can be done, although perhaps not as expeditiously, by an intelligent and conscientious layman. The systems analyst's value, if the services of one are available, would be more pronounced in the later stages of the study. The prime object at this point is to ensure that all the details of the present procedure are brought to light.

We now know WHERE we should start—with the present procedure.

'Start at the Beginning'

At this point it may be as well to elaborate a little further on the interpretation of what is meant by 'start at the beginning'.

In order to consider effective improvements in a procedure, it must be apparent that the present procedure should be thoroughly examined in detail. It should also be realized that a change in one area of a procedure may have a bearing on another part of that, or an adjacent, procedure. But before contemplating any changes surely we must know exactly what is being done at the moment. Otherwise, how can we be certain that what changes may be proposed are actually an improvement on what is already being done at the moment?

Logically, therefore, our starting point must be with the present procedure, and at the very beginning of that procedure. Each step must be taken by itself and thoroughly questioned. But what questions should be asked?

Basic Questions: The basic questions are:

(1) WHY?   e.g. Why need the particular action be done at all, and for what purpose?
(2) WHERE?   e.g. Where, and why that particular location?
(3) WHEN?   e.g. When, and why at that particular time?
(4) BY WHOM?   e.g. By whom, and why that particular person?
(5) HOW?   e.g. Why by that particular method? Why in that particular manner?

In order to illustrate the fact-finding technique, let us assume that an order-invoice-dispatch procedure is under consideration, and that there are three main forms in use: a works order, an invoice, and a dispatch note. The company is a manufacturing organization serving the engineering field.

Although the Order Form must be the first form in the procedure, it should be obvious that before an Order Form can be written up there must be a source document from which the necessary information can be obtained to write up the Order Form.

The fact-finder now knows where to start, and the head of that section is approached to confirm the most suitable time to start with the questioning. The section head and his, or her, section should be aware at this point of the outline of the fact-finder's requirements. Having made the necessary contacts, the operation should begin by the section head being questioned on the general outline of this part of the procedure.

Pattern of Questioning: From this point the fact-finder will proceed to the personnel in the section. How are the orders received? By phone, by post, by salesmen's written orders, by customers calling in person, or by all four methods?

If all four methods are in use, how are orders taken down from the phone and from personal customer approach? Are they time-stamped? Is the initial order scribbled on a pad and then properly written up, or is there a Preliminary Order Form? Is it given a job number at this stage?

Is it a multiple-part form? How many forms are used per day or per week? Are they numbered? Hand-written? Is there any check that orders taken are in fact written up? Do any go astray? How often? How many? Are register machines (continuous forms dispensers) used? Do machines have a locked compartment for a control file copy? If orders are received by salesman's order forms or by post, are they then re-written on a proper form, or is the customer's Purchase Order or the salesman's order form used as source document for later processing operations? Can pricing and extensions be done at this stage? By whom are these operations done? When? How is pricing done—by price lists or by calculation? Who checks prices? *Are* prices checked? How are they checked?

If a proper multiple-part form is used, how many parts does it have? Are good copies obtained? Are the forms easy to write up and to split up? (If possible, have a typical set written up at all points, and watch how this is done. Question any areas of form not written on. Question reasons.) If more than one operator is engaged on this job, check to find out if there are any differences in operation.

What happens to the multiple-part set? If split up, what happens now? Where do all parts go? Are they collected, or are they taken by some member of this department to another location? Why is this done in this manner? (Follow each part later.) Is a file copy kept in the department of origin? How is it filed? What happens to it? Is a file copy necessary for the department? Are all copies necessary?

How are orders despatched? By carrier, by post, by customer, or by all three methods? How does the customer pay? Before or after receiving the goods? On rendering of account? By cash? How is one circumstance distinguishable from another? Is this distinction written in, rubber-stamped, indicated by codes, or are distinctive order forms used?

The personnel should be discreetly asked for their own opinions on how they think their work could be done better. Do they take procedural short-cuts? Why? Are these short-cuts generally used? Do they feel the form could be improved? How? Could the form be re-designed to allow for taking down directly from the phone without first scribbling down information? Would coding or pre-printing of certain items be helpful?

When questioning is finished, the personnel should be thanked for their co-operation and assistance, and credit should be given to them later for any suggestions they make—and they should be made to realize this. Equally they must be reassured that no recriminations will follow whatever they say or divulge—this is not an inquisition. If hostility is met, do not be too quick to demand an answer. Change to another tack, but come back to the original question at a later stage. If still denied an answer, try another source of information—it may be that the person does not wish to show ignorance. Do not use higher authority until absolutely forced. Co-operation in and approval of the project is vital, and it is well worth exercising patience to cultivate them. The objectives have to be sold to these employees, because these are the people who will be asked to operate any amended routine—and there is nothing more difficult to overcome than reluctant allies.

A good selling job at this stage will provide handsome dividends later.

Once this initial stage has been thoroughly checked, and only then, the next section should be decided upon. The subsequent moves will be dictated by the distribution of the original document, whether it is in one section or in multiple parts. If in multiple parts, then each individual part must be followed to its ultimate destination, whether this means it is destroyed or put into a 'permanent' file. If the latter, then find out how permanent this really is.

Since files must be cleared out at some time, find out if the 'permanency' lasts for six months, a year, or two years, or whatever. Question whether this period is long enough, or on the other hand if it is too long. It may be found that there is justification for clearing out documents much more quickly than is being done, thus avoiding cluttering up files unnecessarily. Watch out for the possibility of eliminating the files completely if there is another file elsewhere which could be used for the same purpose. Make notes of these possibilities, and by tactful questioning find out any logical reasons why this second file could not be used.

To avoid becoming involved in diverse forms applications simultaneously, because parallel systems may be in operation, try to ensure that once a form is chosen it is persevered with until each part is fully accounted for. It will be found, for instance, that one or more parts of the original form may be used as source documents for initiating other forms.

Probably practical and physical factors will dictate the next area for investigation following the first phase, but it is as well to check over the notes taken so far to this point to ensure that every operation is clearly stated, because memory can become less sharp as other details of later procedures are accumulated. Being sure of the facts at this point reduces the necessity for unnecessary, and sometimes annoying, re-visits to busy areas.

First Rough Flow-Chart

It is, therefore, advisable at this stage to make a rough flow-chart in order that a visual picture of the overall situation may be obtained at a glance.

Such a chart need only use very simple symbols to indicate basic operations.

It will be realized that words in themselves do tell the story but, of necessity, very slowly. All the information is there, but it can only be assimilated as a succession of little segments, as parts of a mosaic design. On the other hand, a chart, even in a rough form, can present at a glance the whole outline of a procedure, or a part of a procedure.

The chart method of recording a system has many advantages over a written report. At any conference called to discuss and analyse the results of a fact-finding mission such as this, a visual chart on display for all to see makes things infinitely easier for everyone to understand than would sheaves of copious notes. A crucial area can be instantly pinpointed, and all present will be immediately aware, not only of the point being made, but also of the associated areas surrounding it. Possible side effects will be much more apparent, and explanations more quickly understood.

People essentially interpret from their own viewpoint on reading information. They are inclined to overlook other interests, and not to absorb information too deeply if their own particular interests are not under immediate discussion. However, with a chart on display a line of reasoning can be easily and quickly recognized with little or no effort.

Misinterpretation of technical terminology is one of the greatest factors in causing confusion during discussions. This state of affairs is largely avoided by using a chart, as everyone present can actually see not only what is being discussed, but can also see in which area the problem has arisen, and from which point of view the question is being posed.

A further advantage is that after the initial charting of the current procedure a quick means is available of checking against a newly devised procedure, so that advantages can be assessed by almost anyone without undue discussion or deep concentration on written notes. The facility with which such comparisons can be made, now or later, is highly desirable.

Similarly, when the final agreed procedure is charted a permanent record is always on hand, so that a check can be quickly made. Or a further suggested change might be speedily evaluated without the necessity of calling anyone off essential routine work for clarification of details.

The decided advantages of charting a procedure must be very obvious.

There is, however, no intention here of specifying or recommending any one of the numerous methods which are in general use for charting a forms procedure. Many Systems and Procedures Departments use, or have evolved, symbols and methods which they feel are best suited to their requirements, but while they may vary from point to point the basic principles are essentially the same.

There is also no doubt that systems analysts in this field have developed extremely valuable expertise, which should be neither underestimated nor ignored if these services are available. But such assistance may not usually come the way of most, and so a better general understanding of how to undertake simple charting should be of value.

Flow-Charting Symbols

The system shown here has been developed by the author purely with the aim of illustrating the underlying principles of flow-charting clearly to the layman. If an 'accepted' set of symbols is found to be desirable, alternative and widely used systems, some of which present the sequence of operations vertically, can be found described in many good textbooks on Method Study.

Symbols should be developed to denote the few basic operations, and the more simple their construction the more readily can they be used. A template with a minimum of geometrical shapes is very helpful, but the fewer symbols used the better for quick interpretation. By a slight variation to any shape, such as by the addition of a diagonal line or a colour line, many distinctions can be suggested. See Illustration 1.

Illustration 1. Flow-charting symbols

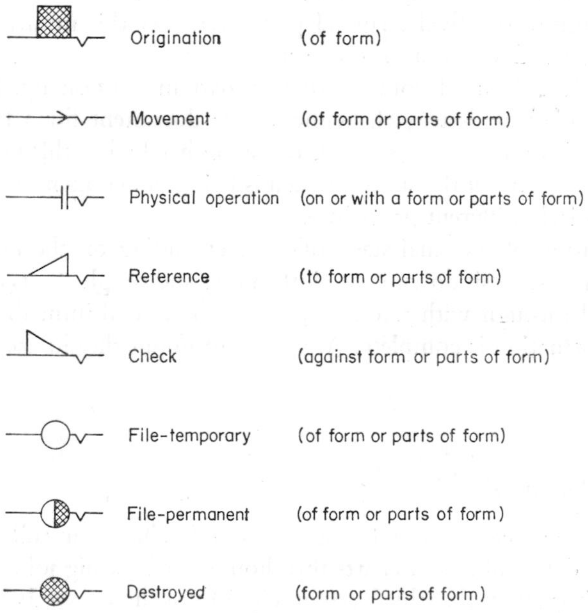

Origination	(of form)
Movement	(of form or parts of form)
Physical operation	(on or with a form or parts of form)
Reference	(to form or parts of form)
Check	(against form or parts of form)
File-temporary	(of form or parts of form)
File-permanent	(of form or parts of form)
Destroyed	(form or parts of form)

So that a brief, condensed account of the particular operation can be made for clarification, it will be found that if a small reverse caret mark is made to join with an elongated panel, then this can contain the necessary data. See Illustration 2.

A good means of making such a flow-chart is to obtain a pack of unprinted but preferably marginally-punched continuous single-sheet stationery, say 10 in (250 mm) wide with a cross-perforation every 11 in (275mm). In this way an unlimited length can be obtained which can not only be finally opened out to show the procedure in a continuous flow, but the pack can also be folded up into a handy size and may even be filed in a binder with flexible nylon posts by means of the marginal holes for ease of reference. By binding across the web of the form pack, two facing pages will show, thus eliminating the need to separate each sheet. Furthermore, by binding in this way the whole continuous chart will remain intact. See Illustration 3.

While it is not always possible, every effort should be made to try to keep a complete operation on one sheet. However, providing the sheets are not separated, little inconvenience will be caused even if the operation continues on to the next sheet.

As previously mentioned, each operation should be roughly sketched out and notations made as described above to ensure that the overall picture of that operation is clearly understood, thus preventing loose ends from being inadvertently overlooked. Only then should the next step of the survey be tackled.

Proceed now in an orderly fashion, covering the path of each part of each set until it comes to a final terminal point, whether this means a permanent file or simply the destruction of the part.

There are situations, of course, where a part may finish up, before being permanently filed or destroyed, as the source document for a further forms application. This must be considered, to establish whether this new form will come into the sphere of the survey which is being undertaken, or whether it is part of an entirely different procedure.

On conclusion of the final stage of the fact-finding on the procedure, the fact-finder must now sit down with all the notes and rough charts of each stage. A quick read-through with references to the charts will immediately indicate if all the information is complete. Any areas of doubt should then be clarified at this point.

Reading the 'Present' Procedure

The present procedure should now be properly charted in full, and from all the collected data and rough charts this should not be a big job.

It is most important that this 'present' chart must show exactly what is really

Illustration 2. Additional instructions

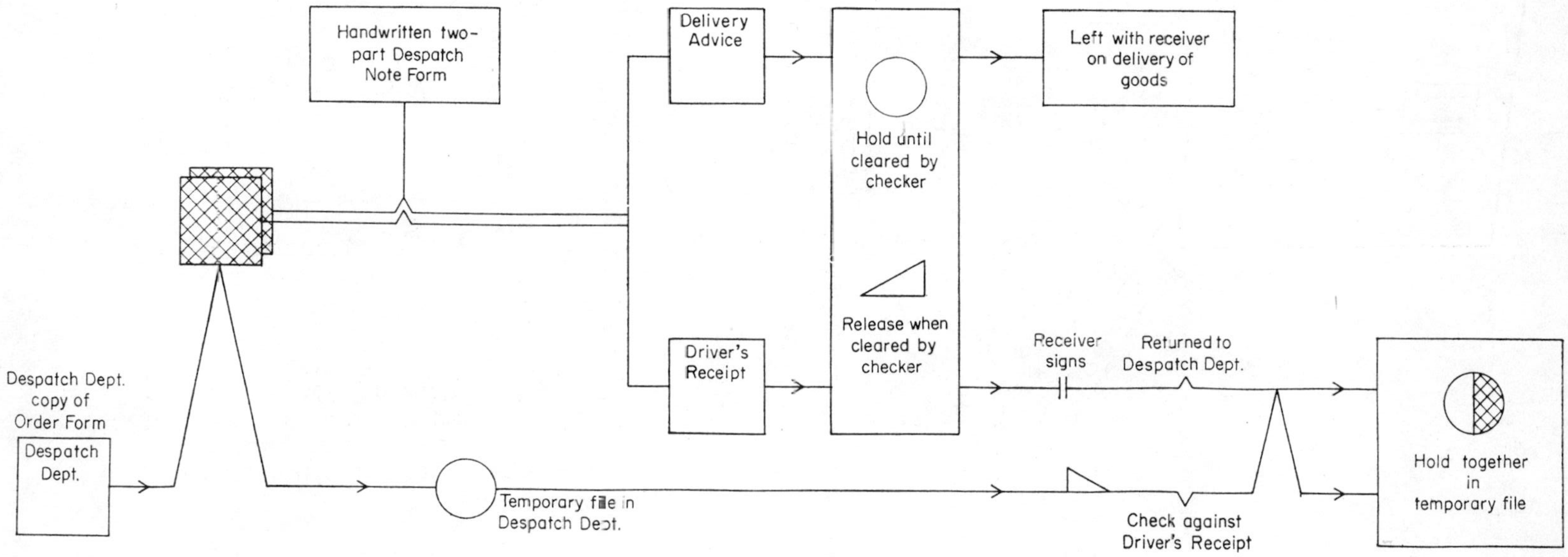

Illustration 3. Continuous pack flow—chart

Where special ruled charting paper is
not available, a good substitute would
be to use a small pack of blank
continuous forms —if possible of 11"
between perforations.
When charting place on top of sheet
ruled with half-inch squares.

in fact being done at present; not what *might* be done, or even what someone *hoped* was being done.

Once this chart has been verified to the fact-finder's satisfaction a meeting must be arranged with all the principals involved, and they should be advised to allow at least two hours to be free from interruption.

In order to avoid waste of time at this stage it should be made clear that control of this meeting must be firmly in the hands of the fact-finder, regardless of whether his superiors are present or not. Otherwise, there is a grave danger of the subsequent discussions wandering considerably from the procedure under review, and the fact-finder is in the best position to decide when a course of discussion should terminate.

Having established this point, the fact-finder, or analyst, should now explain the purpose of the meeting, and the way it will be conducted.

The first step will be that the whole chart will be displayed by pinning to a blackboard or a wall for all to see, and then the *whole* procedure will be traced out by the fact-finder—without comment from the viewers. If someone feels that some clarification is needed on any point or points, he should make notes of such points, because he will be given full opportunity to put questions on the second reading. Even obvious errors should not be commented upon at the first reading. Again, a note should be made to raise the point at the opportune moment.

It is very important that the above manner of conducting this stage of the survey should be adhered to for three good reasons.

First, to save time. Because, if questions are continually asked, the fact-finder can easily lose his train of thought, and digressions will inevitably be made which will divert the other viewers' attention from the overall picture of the procedure. Confusion and resultant loss of interest by many will almost certainly result.

Second, by being allowed to explain the present procedure straight through, the watchers will be assured, and will probably be favourably impressed, by the fact that the analyst does indeed know about the whole procedure. As a result he is more likely to gain the respect of all present, and therefore they will be more likely to accept his direction of the meeting.

Third, it will give all present an insight into other areas about which they may previously have had little or no knowledge. Their awareness may now lead to a frame of mind more conducive to the understanding of the problems of other sections, and it is hoped that a more sympathetic attitude and more enthusiasm will thus be generated for the whole survey project.

On completion of the first reading of the 'present' chart, the analyst should explain the next step. The chart will now be read over, step by step, in a systematic manner, and questions and suggestions will be welcomed—but again, only sequentially on the points on the chart as and when they are reached.

c

Illustration 4. Order—Invoice—Despatch—"Present" procedure. Note: Four forms originated.

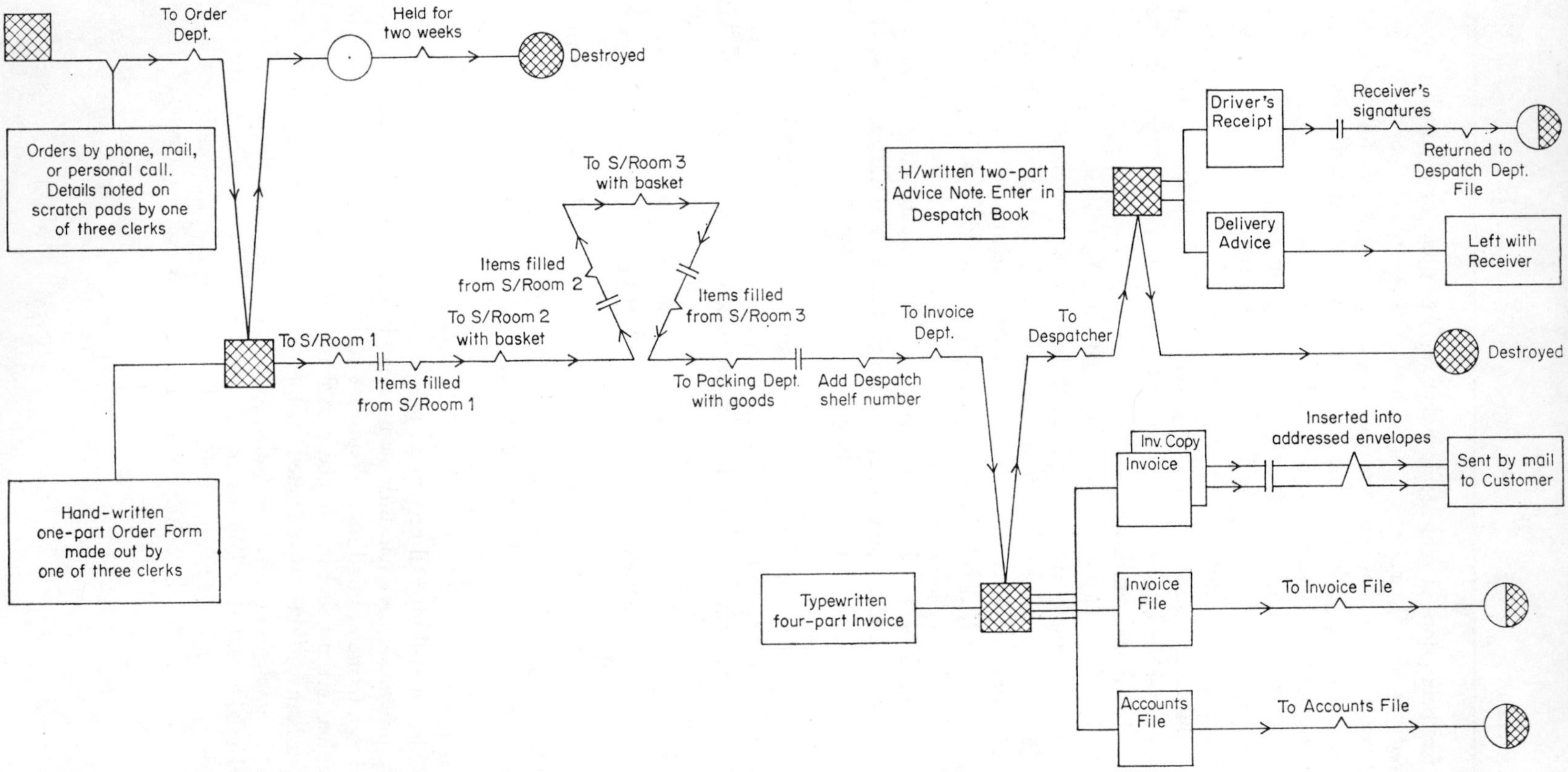

Orders by phone, mail, or personal call. Details noted on scratch pads by one of three clerks

To Order Dept.

Held for two weeks

Destroyed

Hand-written one-part Order Form made out by one of three clerks

To S/Room 1

Items filled from S/Room 1

To S/Room 2 with basket

Items filled from S/Room 2

To S/Room 3 with basket

Items filled from S/Room 3

To Packing Dept. with goods

Add Despatch shelf number

To Invoice Dept.

To Despatcher

H/written two-part Advice Note. Enter in Despatch Book

Driver's Receipt

Receiver's signatures

Returned to Despatch Dept. File

Delivery Advice

Left with Receiver

Destroyed

Typewritten four-part Invoice

Accounts File

To Accounts File

Invoice File

To Invoice File

Invoice

Inv Copy

Inserted into addressed envelopes

Sent by mail to Customer

Illustration 4(a). Preferred Procedure. Note: Two Forms Originated

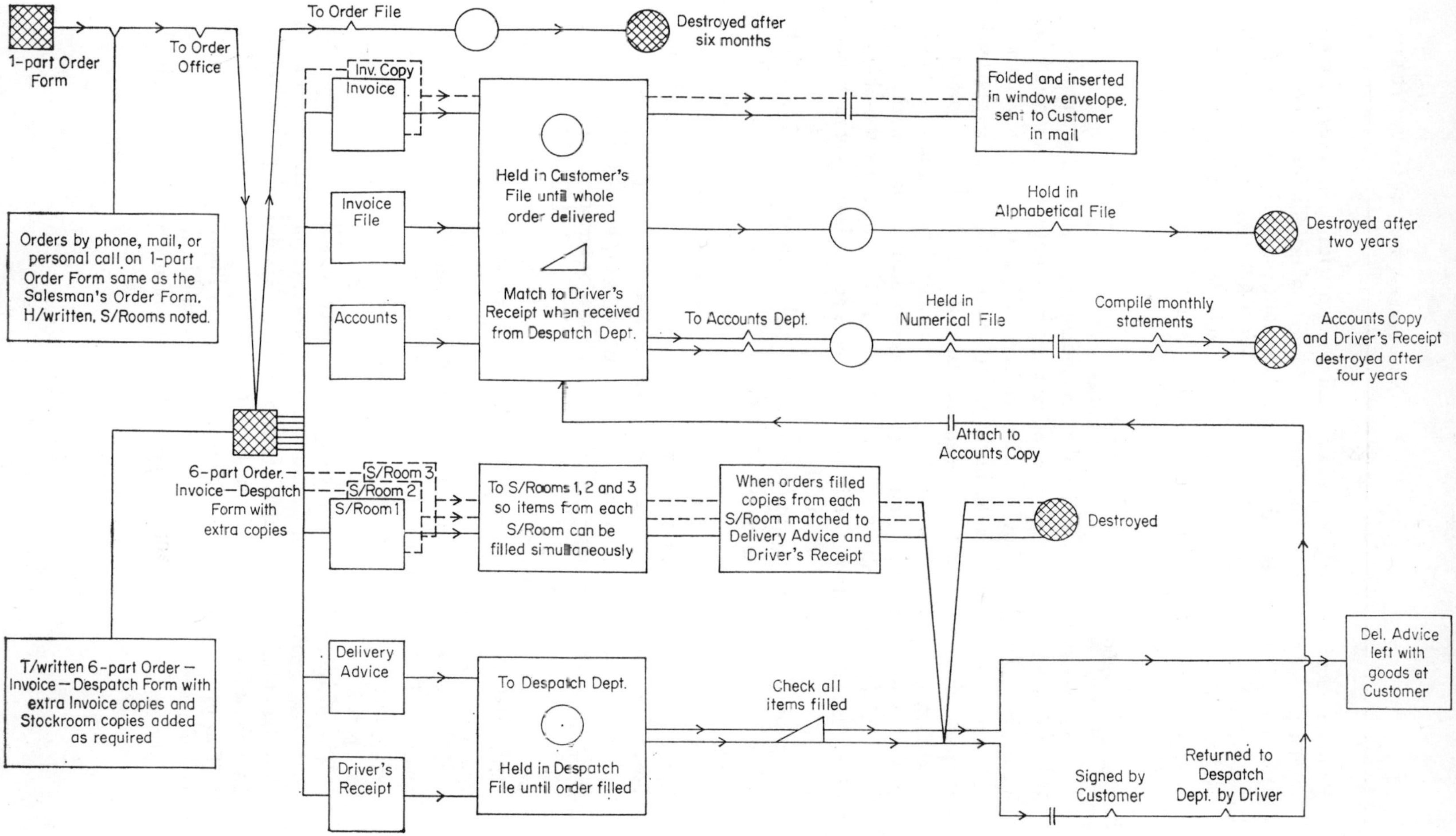

Random questions should be put off until the area with which they are concerned is ready for discussion. Haphazard questioning will almost certainly cause confusion to most and will result in an unwelcome loss of time. The quicker the reading moves along, and the more fully everyone understands each step, the more successful the study and results are likely to be.

For these reasons the analyst must retain a firm hold on the meeting.

Finding the Solutions

It must be assumed that during the fact-finding period the analyst must have received suggestions from the employees on how improvements could be made; and the analyst from his own experience will most probably have some suggestions of his own. It is also likely, and recommended, that he has discussed some or all of these with some of the principals concerned. It is important to discuss such points with at least two other responsible people, because this is indeed a case where two or three heads are better than one. It is amazing how often an apparently brilliant suggestion can be scuttled by a not-too-obvious circumstance. The more experienced heads there are the better, within reason, to watch out for such hidden dangers.

At this point, also, the analyst would be well advised to employ a little salesmanship which, if properly applied, can ease his burden and smooth his path.

Remembering that the people with whom he is dealing may feel some apprehension and have some fears that, somehow, circumstances may be uncovered by this survey which may adversely affect their particular position, it is as well to keep a weather eye open for signs of unreasonable hostility. This can often be identified by an apparent show of unconcern or boredom; an attitude of impatience at this 'waste of time'; or an insistence that there is no 'need' for any changes. One of the strongest indications of this latent fear can be a show of resentment that an 'outsider' is trying 'to show us how to run our section'.

In such circumstances, any show of smug over-confidence on the part of the analyst will almost certainly tend to confirm the above fears. The result may be an almost impenetrable wall of resentment which will make the gaining of co-operation extremely difficult.

The analyst, therefore, will recognize the need to 'sell' confidence to each individual concerned with the survey. Confidence, that is, that what is being done is not only for the benefit of the company, but is also being done by each individual for his own particular benefit.

Too often, however, 'selling' is interpreted as implying that somehow a confidence trick is being played—but nothing could be further from the truth.

True selling is the ability of presenting, for instance as a lawyer might do before a jury, an argument for a course of action which by its logical and reasoned approach will be persuasive enough to be readily understood by, and acceptable to, all concerned. It must be recognized, however, that the manner in which this is done has an enormous bearing on how sympathetically the arguments will be received. There is also no doubt that acceptance is much easier if points of agreement are consolidated and emphasized.

If some thought, therefore, is given to this situation, a pattern of presentation can be seen and established.

The analyst should realize that his own success is dependent on the final result of the survey. That is, through the efforts of the study, either a better procedure will have been developed which is acceptable by all; or, alternatively, the study will have proved beyond doubt that the present system is the best possible under the current circumstances. Success in a study should never be judged on the number of changes introduced—but purely on the efficiency of the system eventually decided upon, with or without changes.

The analyst should, therefore, be wary of demonstrating how clever and ingenious he is by taking credit for suggested improvements. There are two very solid reasons why he should be careful about his attitude here, as his prime object is only to get such improvements accepted if they are of value.

First, and probably most important, is the possibility that if the analyst's suggestion is made with lack of tact, whoever may be responsible for that particular area or section may easily regard this as a criticism, and instinctively antagonism will be felt towards the suggestion—possibly even more strongly if the suggestion is a good one, as the person concerned may feel that his ability has been challenged.

Second, if the suggestion has been badly presented and reason is found to suspect that the suggestion is not workable, then—people being very human— the destruction of the idea may be welcomed with great satisfaction. This, of course, will do the analyst's image no good at all—and may, in fact, put the success of the whole study in jeopardy.

If the proposals, however, come from personnel themselves, then not only will the aforementioned fears be avoided but the final adoption of these proposals, if approved, are much less likely to encounter opposition since they, themselves, made the suggestions—and will, of course, receive the credit.

Bearing this in mind, and also keeping in mind that reasonably intelligent people are being dealt with, be wary of preceding a suggestion with 'I suggest that . . . the following would be an improvement.'

A more acceptable approach would be to introduce the proposal into the general discussion at an approriate time by perhaps starting with, 'Well, is there another way of doing this?' Then by a loose outline of what is in mind, encourage discussions along these lines until the logic of the suggestion begins to become apparent. Once someone catches on to the purpose of the proposal,

it is a simple matter then to amplify by saying, 'As Mr Brown has pointed out
. . . this could be hand-written instead of being typewritten . . .', etc. It is then
timely to enter enthusiastically into *support of Mr Brown's proposal.*

By using this approach, finally there are placed before the meeting a number
of proposals from the people actively involved in the operating of the system—
and not suggestions from an 'outsider'. The chances of success must be improved.

The greatest 'sales aid' for any salesman is the ability to present the means
for a customer to sell himself. After all, the salesman does not make the final
decision; the customer does—but only after he has convinced himself that this
action is the right one. Therefore, allow people to convince themselves by
simply providing the means for them to do so.

The final bonus is, of course, the fact that all personnel will be inclined to
ensure the success of a procedure which they can feel they helped to develop,
and for which they may have been given an 'honourable mention'.

The ultimate object of the project, an improved procedure which is generally
acceptable to all concerned, will be more likely to be attained.

Questioning the Procedure

Questioning of each part of the present procedure should begin with the
second reading of the chart.

The fact-finder should again guide and prompt the questioning of each facet
of every operation, particularly in areas that may have been previously overlooked. As in his fact-finding mission, the routine questions relating to Why?
Where? When? By Whom? and How? should be applied to all operations.

By reference to the chart and by listening to the subsequent discussions a
promising suggestion can be quickly spotted and noted down. The idea can then
be elaborated on, and the 'pros and cons' quickly assessed. Agreement can be
quickly obtained regarding the value of making changes. To encourage close
questioning it may be as well to examine the probabilities and possibilities
which might be expected to arise from a thorough investigation.

If we keep in mind our purpose, which is at least to reduce the volume of
'wasted time that does not pile up in great heaps on the floor', we should recognize what we hope will arise from our basic questions.

The following may help to indicate what might be anticipated from our
questions:

Why? This question is designed to establish whether or not it is absolutely
necessary to do this operation at all. Is the information already available from
another source? Is this something that is being done elsewhere, and therefore
in this instance could it be eliminated? Is this operation something that could

be done equally well, or better, at another point or by another person? Could it be done at the same time as another operation of a similar nature, thus eliminating unnecessary duplication of this operation? What benefit derives from this operation? Could further benefits be enjoyed if the scope of the operation was increased, or reduced?

Where? Why is it done in this location? Could it be done better elsewhere? If the present is best location, is excessive walking or movement involved? Could this be reduced or eliminated by a change of location? Would these changes make a significant improvement in performance? Would change of location produce complications elsewhere?

How? This is an extremely important area for producing improvements, and it may be profitable to list some of these probabilities in sections, taking writing methods as an example.

(*a*) *Hand-Written:* How is this done? Is information written on a scrap of paper, then re-written on a designed multiple-part form? Would it be simpler to type it straight away? Would time be saved if a form was made with pre-printed items which only requires ticking or insertion of quantities? If hand-written, are the multiple-part forms in loose sets, in pads, or in continuous packs (for use in a forms-dispenser register machine)? If loose sets, are they written in one or many locations? What surface is available for writing on— a desk, a writing plate, a clip-board with fold-over writing plate? If clip-board, how many forms does this hold, is there a fold-over writing plate, and is there any facility for keeping a copy if set is split up? If pads, does this involve insertion of loose carbons? Would matters be speeded up and information made clearer if forms were made of self-copying papers, or interleaved with one-time carbons, with a fold-over cover as a writing plate? If a register machine is used, is this a portable model for carrying about in the hand? Does it have a compartment for holding the writer's copy? Since larger packs could then be used, would a counter-top model be better? Would an electric rather than a manual model be warranted? If a counter-top model is presently in use, would portable models be more useful—perhaps thus eliminating a bottleneck caused by fixed location machines?

(*b*) *Type-Written:* Would it be more effective, if acceptable, to hand-write this document? If typewriting multiple copies, are these single sheets into which carbons are being inserted and then removed by hand?

This is an area which should be looked at very closely, particularly if the annual usage of these forms is 10,000 or more. It should be noted that with a 7-part glued-stub set, for instance, non-productive time in the typing operation can be reduced in many cases to one-tenth of a similar operation which calls for the hand-insertion and hand-removal of carbon papers. Great economies can often be made here.

If the annual usage of the form under consideration is greater than 20,000 forms, would continuous forms significantly improve the rate of typing by virtually eliminating most non-productive movements? Furthermore, if two or more typists are engaged full-time in processing these continuous forms, would the circumstances warrant manual or electric line-finders? This device is geared to advance the form vertically to the next writing-line position. For example, in an invoice form it would advance from the last address-line straight to the first writing-line position in the body of the form; then from the last body entry straight to the first address-line of the next form by means of a lever or key—all intermediate skips being fully automatic.

Would a re-design of the form reduce typing time? Is the source document for this form designed in a manner that will ensure the most efficient transference of data from the source document to this form—or does the typist have to search all over the document, thus wasting time, to find the necessary information for typing? (Apart from time saved, the possibility of transcription errors can be reduced if the source document is properly designed.) Similarly, if this document is to be used as a source for a subsequent form, is it properly designed with the object in mind of ensuring maximum efficiency for informational retrieval required by the next operation?

There are also many refolding, decollating, and carbon-removal pieces of equipment which can improve the performance of typing operations—and these should be kept in mind for consideration.

(c) *Duplicators:* There is a tremendous range of duplicating and photo-copying equipment which might be considered for reducing bottlenecks and waste of time. It is beyond the range of this text to enumerate the scope and variety of this type of office equipment. The introduction of such, or any, of these office machines would be dependent upon resources and many other factors which would require to be carefully considered. It is enough to mention that with some of this equipment a master sheet can be introduced into a multiple part set, thus eliminating wasteful duplication of typing operations. Where such a possibility does exist, be sure that attention is given to such a time-saver.

This is one example where by increasing the immediate cost of a business form, a real saving can be made in a later stage of the system—a saving which can be many times more valuable than the extra initial expense. In this matter, equipment manufacturers and business forms suppliers will be pleased to offer experienced advice and assistance if problems arise in such a situation. Be careful if duplicate copies are required to be obtained from one copy of the form, as some self-copying images are not acceptable to certain duplicating equipment—particularly if the image is pale in colour.

(d) *General Office Writing Equipment:* Here again, there is a prolific range of equipment, and a bewildering number of models within each range. They have varying capacities, sizes, and prices which can only be assessed from each individual need, potential, and financial viewpoint.

In this area, the only general advice which can be offered is that attention should be paid to the design of the form being used to ensure that the source document should be related in design as far as possible to the form being processed. If the form itself is also to be used as a source document for a subsequent form, then this latter should also share a relationship of design. Care should also be taken, where the number of parts of a form has been increased due to a change in procedure, that write-tests are made to establish that the resultant copies are as clear and legible as is required.

A very common and costly fault arises from increasing the number of copies beyond the limits of the original copying agent—be it one-time carbon or self-copying paper.

(e) *Addressing Machines:* Once again, there are many makes and models, in both manual and electric types, and proper consideration must be given to probable individual requirements before coming to any decision.

Again, be careful to make thorough write-tests with the form if changing from manual type to an electric model, as there is a difference of impression in the impact action of the usual manual addressing machine to the roller action of most electric models. Checks must be made with the form to ensure that adequate copy-through is obtained with the new machine.

This could involve a change in the quality of the one-time carbon being used, or could cause a reduction in the number of copies possible if self-copying paper is used. In any event, do not overlook these possibilities, but insist on tests being satisfactorily conducted.

(f) *Labelling:* If there is a call for a quantity of labels because a number of parcels or packages or boxes are required in one shipment, do not overlook the possibility of including a master stencil label in the form-set used for dispatch papers. This type of stencil master can be 'cut' simultaneously with the original typing. The master stencil is then fitted to a hand-stamp with ink-pad and can provide a considerable number of impressions. The number of impressions, of course, will be governed by how receptive is the proposed surface to be labelled. This can be a valuable time-saver, and is well worth consideration.

When? Is this operation one that could be held until a group of similar operations can be done at the same time? Thus perhaps reducing continual re-adjusting or re-setting of equipment? Alternatively, would bottlenecks at another point be reduced or eliminated if this operation is performed immediately it arises? Would the performance of this operation be more advantageous at one certain time rather than at another time?

By Whom? Have the personnel who perform this function been specially trained for this position? Would specialist training improve their performance? Why were they chosen for the job? Was it simply because they were on the spot? Are they aware of the importance of their job? Have they been made aware of the use which will be made of their efforts? Could instruction improve the amount of information they might be able to obtain? Are they aware of the problems which might arise if the job is not done with maximum efficiency?

It is not possible to compile an entirely complete list of questions which could be asked because the permutations of personnel, probabilities, possibilities, equipment, and differing circumstances are virtually infinite. But there is no doubt that a study of the foregoing will indicate a pattern for the questioning technique.

Objectives

The object is clear—the need to be aware of the true situation. With the real facts and a detailed knowledge of the system under consideration, improvements, if any, can be much more quickly and easily introduced than would be the case if the administrators were floundering about in a morass of misinformation, rumour, and ignorance.

No doubt, some extra effort may be called for at this stage, but the value of the possible efficiencies usually more than justify the work entailed by the study. Success seldom comes without effort.

The Final Phase

Little mention has been made up to this point about re-designing of existing forms, and the creation of new forms, which will almost certainly have arisen during discussion in the earlier phases. This omission has been deliberate, so that the survey project could be explained without digression into the considerable complexities of form design. As will be found, however, the latter part of this text will be given over entirely to the basic approaches to good form design, with advice on how this can best be incorporated for maximum efficiency.

Having obtained final agreement on what changes should be made in the procedure and how these changes should be implemented, the final phase of the survey is now approaching—that is, the charting of the 'proposed' system.

Before starting the actual charting the analyst should go over all the points, preferably with the office manager who will give the final approval, to ensure that there are no loose ends.

Having verified all the relevant facts and information, including the new or revised forms pertaining to the proposed procedure, the analyst can now proceed with the final chart in a manner similar to the orginal 'present' chart.

Since agreement will already have been reached on the system, and in view of the knowledge and experience gained on the first chart, little time need be spent on this step.

It might be added, however, that no delay should be made in producing the chart, as it is a good axiom 'to strike while the iron is hot' and thus take full advantage of enthusiasm already generated. To delay the chart for any length of time is to invite the possibility of having to re-persuade the already-persuaded.

On completion of the 'proposed' system chart, the major participants should again be assembled for the final reading. This procedure should be that which applied to the reading of the original chart.

Again, the analyst or fact-finder must be in complete charge of the meeting. A complete read-through of the new chart must be permitted without interruption. To prevent attention from wandering, it is advisable to have only the new chart on display at the first read-through. Then, before the second read-through, and the subsequent clarifications, it can be advantageous to put up the old procedure chart also.

Questions should now be invited, as clarification of points can be simply made with the two charts on display. Improvements can be quickly and clearly illustrated, and it will be found that many misapprehensions and much confused thinking will be eliminated.

Emphasis should again be laid on the point that this system under review is a result of the participation and involvement of all the people present, and it should be stressed that the successful implementation of the system is now the direct responsibility of each of them.

Allow full, but controlled, discussion until everyone is satisfied with this second chart. Minor modifications may be raised, but if the survey has been conducted properly little should now require to be changed.

It only remains for the office manager, or the senior company officer present, to close the exercise by expressing pleasure for the co-operation, enthusiasm, and assistance rendered by all concerned with the development of the new procedure.

If conducted in the manner indicated in the foregoing, successive studies will be made more simple because of this experience and, in fact, they may be confidently welcomed by all parties involved.

2 CONSTRUCTION

Definition: BUSINESS FORM: *business*—n., occupation for a livelihood; *form*—n., method of arrangement of details.

THE PURPOSE OF A BUSINESS FORM

The general term 'business form' has developed through common usage, although a more accurate term might have been 'business-like form', since the definition from the dictionary shows this to be—*business-like*; a., practical, methodical, systematic; and *form*; n., method of arrangement of details. Thus, a business-like form would be a 'practical, methodical, systematic method of arrangement of details'.

Here, then, lies the definition of the purpose of any business form no matter how simple or basic the form appears to be.

Regrettably, too often this essential definition of a business form is not fully understood—and in many cases is not even considered at all. It must be clearly understood that business forms cannot be judged by the ordinary standards which would normally apply to most other printed products. When finally printed, the job is *not* done—the form must still *function*. Only after its functional ability has been demonstrated can an opinion be expressed as to whether a form is effective or otherwise.

The capacity of a form to function with maximum efficiency is much more likely if the originator has a clear and detailed understanding of the purpose for which the form was designed, as well as a thorough knowledge of the circumstances under which the document will be processed.

The basic objective of any forms originator should be to ensure, in a business form, a construction and design that will adequately and efficiently provide scope for maximum information with minimum effort required for documentation in relation to handling processes, source documents, and requirements of information retrieval. This can only be accomplished if there is a full and complete understanding of the whole system under consideration.

Too often a form is produced for a basic purpose with little or no regard to source documents or requirements of information retrieval. A result can be that a subsequent system or procedure may become unnecessarily complex and complicated; as in the case, say, where a poorly planned form is being used as a source document for a punched-card application. Few forms stand on their own, and in general most forms are to some extent inter-dependent on other forms or procedures. They must, therefore be designed with this in mind—and only a thorough knowledge and understanding of the whole procedure can ensure maximum functional efficiency in a form.

FUNCTIONAL ABILITY

Functional ability is dependent upon a considerable number of factors, not least of which will be the actual design of the form. Basically, three main objectives must be kept in mind before form-design is undertaken: (1) ease of documentation; (2) information-storage capacity; (3) ease of information-retrieval.

It is, therefore, entirely inadequate to judge a newly printed form simply on the basis of the opinion that 'it looks all right'—although the aesthetic appearance can in itself be a psychological factor in ensuring maximum functional ability.

To ensure this functional effectiveness it may be as well to elaborate on these three basic objectives required in the design of a business form.

1. *Ease of Documentation*

As was mentioned in the survey section, the most suitable method of writing should have been decided upon; i.e., handwriting, typing, accounting machine, tabulator, computer, addressing machine, etc. In addition to, and in conjunction with, this aspect of the operation, the circumstances of the writing must also be considered. The operation must be performed in the most efficient sequence in relation to the data or information concerned, both with regard to any source document being used to complete the document and with consideration for requirements of information-retrieval from the document.

This should imply that the sequence of data should be laid down in the manner which has been found to be most suitable for all related documents. The purpose of this is, of course, to make the transference of information from one document to another as systematic and simple as possible in order to reduce the time factor involved on each form. Furthermore, if the transference of information is done sequentially then the possibility of transcription errors can be substantially reduced. Checking becomes much more simple if sequential data are available than would be the case if the information was scattered all over the source document.

The need for correlation of design in associated forms can now be seen to be desirable for maximum efficiency.

In general, every effort should be made to group related information in close proximity, in order that there need be no hesitation in recognizing which area of the form will contain required information.

For example, if you have a combined invoice-dispatch form showing the 'Invoice to' address at top left and the 'Ship to' address at top right, then an attempt should be made to show the customer's account no., customer's order no., and date at the left of the form. Similarly, consignment note no., name of carrier, and dispatch date should be kept to the right-hand side of the form.

Because of complicating factors this may not always be possible, but some thought should certainly be given to such points, as demonstrated in Illustrations 5 and 5(a).

Illustration 5. Combined Invoice/Despatch Form — Undesirable design, though appearance good.

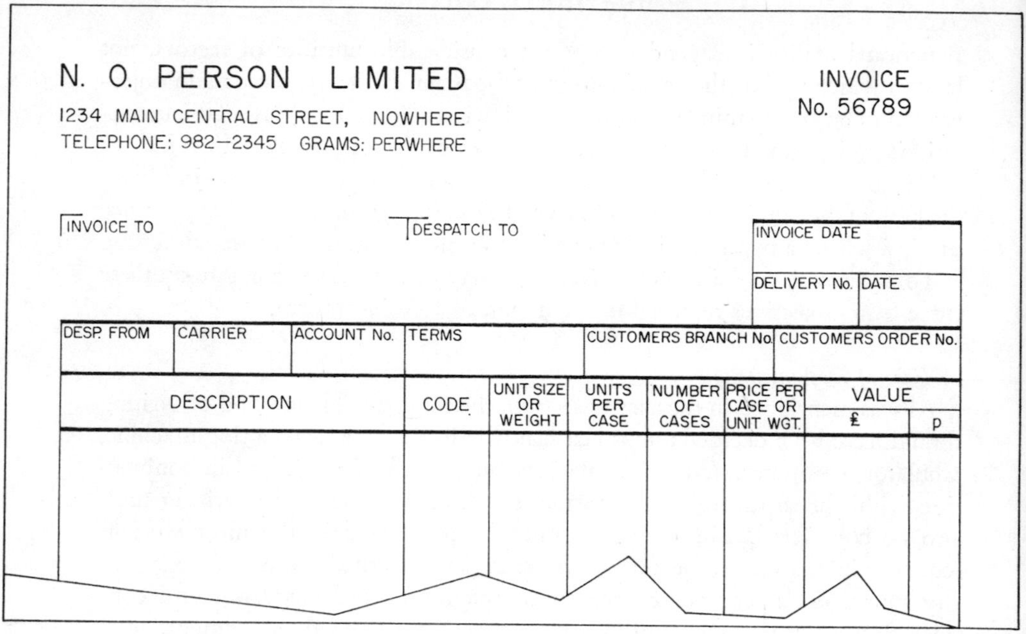

N. O. PERSON LIMITED

1234 MAIN CENTRAL STREET, NOWHERE
TELEPHONE: 982–2345   GRAMS: PERWHERE

INVOICE
No. 56789

INVOICE TO

DESPATCH TO

INVOICE DATE		
DELIVERY No.	DATE	

DESP. FROM	CARRIER	ACCOUNT No.	TERMS		CUSTOMERS BRANCH No.	CUSTOMERS ORDER No.

DESCRIPTION	CODE	UNIT SIZE OR WEIGHT	UNITS PER CASE	NUMBER OF CASES	PRICE PER CASE OR UNIT WGT.	VALUE	
						£	p

Illustration 5(a). Combined Invoice/Despatch Form — Preferred design, good appearance.

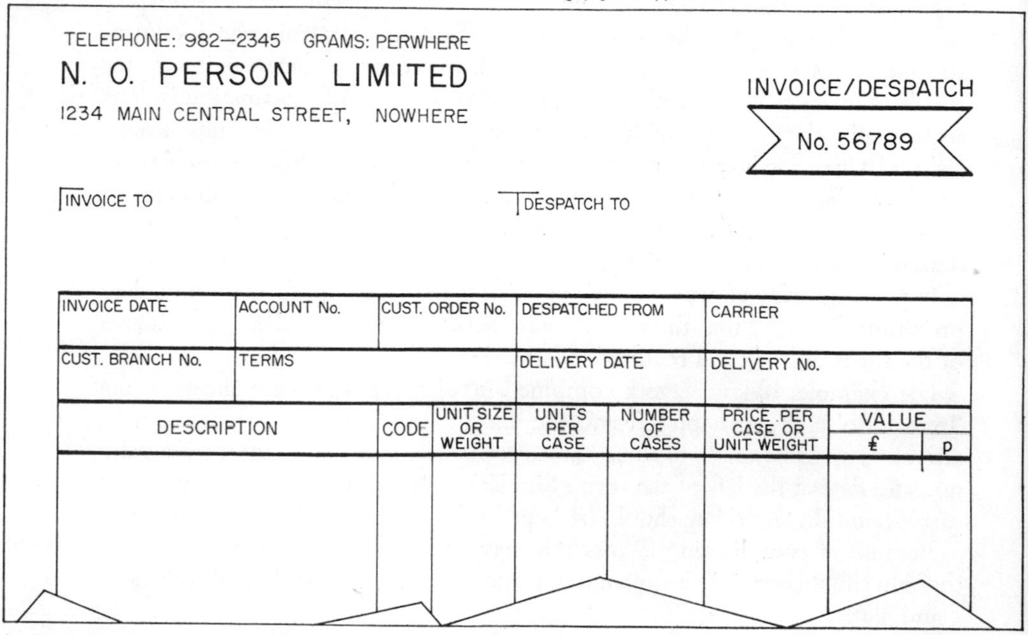

TELEPHONE: 982–2345   GRAMS: PERWHERE

N. O. PERSON LIMITED

1234 MAIN CENTRAL STREET, NOWHERE

INVOICE/DESPATCH

No. 56789

INVOICE TO

DESPATCH TO

INVOICE DATE	ACCOUNT No.	CUST. ORDER No.	DESPATCHED FROM	CARRIER
CUST. BRANCH No.	TERMS		DELIVERY DATE	DELIVERY No.

DESCRIPTION	CODE	UNIT SIZE OR WEIGHT	UNITS PER CASE	NUMBER OF CASES	PRICE PER CASE OR UNIT WEIGHT	VALUE	
						£	p

Generally, a hand-written form may allow a little more latitude than is possible in the more precise form-design demanded by typewritten documents or those used in data-processing equipment. Nevertheless, while there is less of a problem when handwriting because less effort is required to move up, down, or across the form, it must be agreed that a systematic sequence of writing will obviously increase speed and ease of documentation.

Check-Boxes: A useful means of saving space and time, whatever the writing method, lies in the judicious use of check-boxes.

Where common items or instructions apply, the possibility of using abbreviated descriptions above check-boxes can often save lengthy and unnecessarily time-consuming writing or typing.

While this method is often used for lists of stock items on order forms or inventory control sheets, it is not always realized that by applying a little thought to the problem many other uses can be made of it. An example would be in indicating specific instructions on works instructions sheets, etc. Invoice forms can use this device to confirm credit ratings or categories, or to indicate dispatch procedures relevant to customers' collections or to specific carriers.

Code Columns: Where a multiplicity of alternatives exists, of course, a more sophisticated method, such as a coding system, may be worth examination.

The code, whether alphabetical, numerical, or alpha-numerical, may be printed on the face of the form—either in close proximity to the 'code' column, or on otherwise unused space such as on the stub or the finger-grip portion of a snap-apart set. See Illustrations 6 and 6(a).

If too extensive for face-printing, the full code could be back-printed—on perhaps only one controlled copy, if there is any question of security of the code.

If back printing is contemplated for any reason whatever, ensure that only the weak colours such as grey, pale green, or pale blue are used, otherwise annoyance and inconvenience could be caused by 'show-through'—particularly if the printing of the particular part or parts is done on thin stock.

A little thought, in view of the complexities of circumstances surrounding the design of any form, can usually result in ideas being incorporated into the layout of a form which will improve the ease of documentation. Such improvements can frequently contribute significantly to the efficiency of a whole procedure—and when such efficiencies are taken over an annual period and translated into a relative cash figure it can often be astonishing how valuable the improvements are.

Such exercises will quickly provide proof that the true cost of a business form must include the cost of handling and processing that form—and cost must not be simply considered as only the purchase price of the form compared to another price.

Illustration 6. Code—printed on stub

DISCOUNT CODE	▶ A – NO DISCOUNT	B – WITHIN 30 DAYS 1%	C – WITHIN 14 DAYS $2\frac{1}{2}$%
	D – WITHIN 7 DAYS 5%	E – SPECIAL DISCOUNT	F – TRADE $12\frac{1}{2}$%

W. E. R. NOBODY LIMITED,
321 ANY STREET · ANYWHERE

INVOICE

No. 87654

⌐INVOICE TO   ⌐DESPATCH TO

L   ⌐

QUANTITY	D E S C R I P T I O N	UNIT PRICE	CODE	EXTENSION £ l p

T O T A L

Now, consider what should be on the form.

2. *Information Storage Capacity*

This relates to more than just the size of the form itself. Many factors are involved. Basically, a decision must be made as to what information must be accommodated for the primary function of the document—then further consideration must be given to ensure that adequate, but not wasteful, space is given to the various columns, boxes, etc.

For example, never allow $\frac{1}{2}$ in or $\frac{3}{4}$ in (15–20 mm) for an obvious two-digit column, such as a pence or a cent column. Similarly, with code columns, never allow more than a one-digit space on both sides of a code in a known-maximum digit column.

While the required space may be more difficult to ascertain in a hand-written form, if a *reasonable* space is shown people will generally reduce their writing to allow for the permitted space.

With most typewriting or other mechanical writing processes, however,

Illustration 6(a). Code—at foot

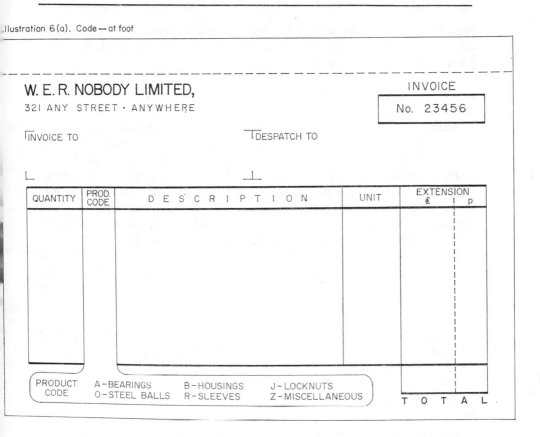

W. E. R. NOBODY LIMITED,
321 ANY STREET · ANYWHERE

INVOICE
No. 23456

INVOICE TO

DESPATCH TO

QUANTITY	PROD. CODE	D E S C R I P T I O N	UNIT	EXTENSION £	p

PRODUCT CODE A-BEARINGS   B-HOUSINGS   J-LOCKNUTS
O-STEEL BALLS   R-SLEEVES   Z-MISCELLANEOUS

T O T A L

more precise specifications can be assessed, as the 'pitch' and 'throw' of the machines will be known factors, whether the measurements are in inch units or those of the metric system. An actual count will establish exactly how much space is required for each column. Also to be borne in mind is the form's relation to adjacent documents.

Ascertaining Form Size

Width: Factors which may require recognition as having a bearing on the final size may include a company policy of standardization of form sizes for filing convenience; relation of proposed size to allow economical cuts from standard paper reel widths or standard paper sheet sizes; and the necessity of using specific sizes for mechanical equipment such as pinwheel or friction-fed forms dispensers (autographic registers), pinwheel platens on typewriters, or other devices.

If, for one reason or another, the function of the form is being extended to

D

permit inclusion of additional data, then this will also need to be measured to allow for inclusion. In fact, only after this has been done can consideration be given to the overall size of the document.

Depth: The depth of the form, which controls the number of writing lines, is frequently given scant attention when considering the actual requirements of information-storage capacity of the form. On many occasions the depth of the form is decided upon for no better reason than that it is a 'standard' depth. A little study will often prove, however, that the form is much deeper than is really required. This adds to the inefficiencies, by costing more to purchase; by taking up unnecessary storage space before use; and, after initial processing, by occupying more space than necessary in filing cabinets, both temporary and permanent. A further cost factor involved is that larger, and therefore more expensive, filing equipment than is really necessary is called for.

The problem of deciding on the depth of a new form may prove a difficult one, unless previous experience or tangible evidence exists as a guide. In the event of a new form a considered estimate of information capacity requirements must be made, taking all known factors into consideration.

Re-designed Forms: If, on the other hand, the form has already been in use and is simply being re-designed, then the solution of the depth problem is much easier to ascertain.

In the case of a previously used form, such as an invoice, take the files for an average three-month period, or better still a six-month period, and make a line-count of the lines in the 'body' area of the form.

This operation can be simplified by the use of an appropriately calibrated ruler, in sixths of inches or millimetres, or as required for local linear standards. In this way single-spacing, space-and-half, or double-spacing can be easily coped with.

It can now be established what is the average number of lines written per document for comparison with the greatest number of lines for which space has been allowed. It is now also a simple matter to show as a percentage the number of forms carrying less than the average number of lines, and also those carrying more than average. The latter can be classified as 1-over average, 2-over, 3-over, etc.

An analysis should now be made to establish a suitable depth, having taken into account the varying factors to be considered, which would permit the typing of the routine information in, say, 97 per cent or so of such documents.

It will be found that only a few documents really require more than the space decided upon for such a calculated depth. Furthermore, if these occasions are in the region of only $2\frac{1}{2}$ to 3 per cent of the annual forms consumption, then it may be found that the overall saving in cost and efficiency of the smaller form well justifies the fact that an extra $2\frac{1}{2}$ to 3 per cent of these documents may have to be typed on two forms.

It is also possible, of course, that the reverse situation may be disclosed and, in fact, a too high proportion of the documents are required to be typed on two forms. The solution here would be to increase efficiency by increasing the depth.

This area, however, is well worth investigation in multiple-part forms, as the value of stationery stocks constitutes a considerable part of the cost of business forms.

If even 3 in (75 mm) can be reduced from the depth of an 8 in × 10 in (200 × 250 mm) form, then 24 sq. in (1·5 dm²) or 30 per cent, are thus saved on one part alone. If the set is a six-part self-copying one, the saving is 144 sq. in (9 dm²) per set. On a moderate annual usage of 50,000 sets the saving is 7,200,000 sq. in (4,500 m²)—or the equivalent of sufficient paper for an additional 21,400 new sets! If this is worked out as a cost figure, a worthwhile target can be seen.

Pre-printed Time-Savers

Information-storage capacity can also be increased by other means, such as the saving of not only typing time but in the saving of space on the form by pre-printing items over check-boxes which merely require to be marked by an 'X' or other symbols.

Another simple device which can be incorporated as a space- and time-saver arises where a 'yes' or 'no' decision is called for. Instead of two check boxes, only print one—with instructions to check with an 'X' if affirmative and to leave blank if negative, or vice-versa. See Illustrations 7 and 7(a).

Illustration 7. Two check boxes   Illustration 7(a). Preferred one box

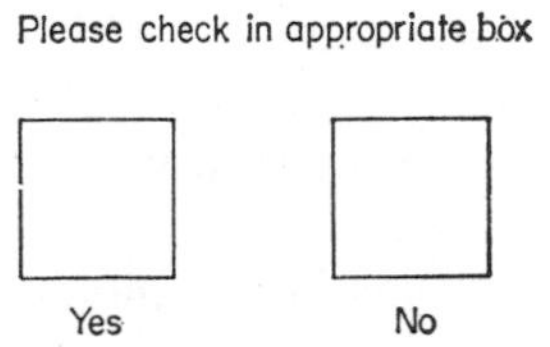

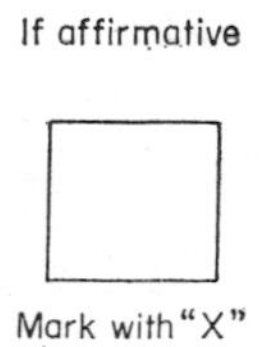

Please check in appropriate box   If affirmative

Yes   No   Mark with "X"

A little thought can often reveal many other ways of increasing capacity without necessarily increasing the form size, particularly by simple redesigning to use up neglected space.

3. Ease of Information-Retrieval

In view of the foregoing it will be assumed that this basic consideration will now have been taken into account. Similar requirements in form-design will apply to ensure maximum efficiency of this form in relation to, and in conjunction with, associated documents which have or require common data.

Again, detailed information regarding the purpose, usage, and handling of the document is vital before commencing the design, or redesign, of such a form.

A Business-Like Form

It may become increasingly clear that a business form will only be as efficient as its construction and design permits—and the efficiency of a procedure itself depends heavily on the related forms.

In order to ensure that every effort will be made to secure maximum efficiency in the form, a systematic and methodical approach to all the problems involved should be made—in a similar manner to that which was used when approaching the system itself.

To this end an attempt will be made to illustrate and elaborate on the construction and design of forms in general, so that a correct mental approach can be acquired to deal even with the unusual circumstances which will arise from time to time.

We might also consider more closely the reasons why we should have made-up sets at all.

Basically, of course, we require multiple copies of information for various valid reasons which will be readily understood by all. In order to get copies at one writing, and thus avoid endless wasteful duplication of effort, we must have a method of obtaining copies of the original writing, and this can be done by inserting by hand a sheet of carbon between each sheet of paper, by which means the necessary impressions are obtained. Self-duplicating papers have now been developed, and these will be considered also. However, carbon paper is still the most widely used means of copying so this process will be considered first.

To process forms comprising loose paper parts and loose carbons many non-productive actions are involved, so let us observe the sequence for a typing operation.

(*a*) The correct number of sheets and correct number of pieces of carbon paper must be collected.

(*b*) The carbon must then be placed in position by hand, one sheet at a time.

(*c*) Care must be taken in jogging papers and carbons together, particularly if sheets are ruled in columns or have ruled boxes, in order that the sheets are in true alignment with one another.

(*d*) The loose set must be inserted into the machine.

(*e*) Once in the typewriter, care must again be taken to ensure exact alignment, as these loose sheets can be easily moved out of register.

(*f*) Turn platen to first typing line and first typing position.

(*g*) Actual typing operation.

(*h*) Remove loose sets from machine.

(*i*) Remove carbons one by one by hand, or try to shake loose if carbon is corner-cut to permit this. However, because of the indentation caused by the typing, added to the natural adhesion of the carbon, shaking out is an untidy operation at best.

As can be easily seen, most of the above movements are wasteful and non-productive. In fact, only (*g*) is productive.

To illustrate, if a seven-part set is taken, with six carbons interleaved, it will be found that under moderately normal conditions the above operation, excluding the one productive movement of typing, will take approximately 60 seconds.

If, however, there is a glued-stub 'snap-apart' set of seven parts and six carbons (or any number for that matter), the non-productive time will be reduced to approximately 6 seconds, because the only motions here are: (*a*) insert in typewriter, (*b*) turn to first writing line and position, (*c*) type, (*d*) remove, and (*e*) tear apart in one movement.

To take this point a little further, if we assume that the average time for processing each document is five minutes, and a typist spends all her time typing such forms, then we can see that we can have a potential increase in her output of at least 18 per cent by using a glued snap-apart set in place of loose sheets and carbons!

Alternatively, by taking the typist's annual salary, plus overhead expenses at roughly 40 per cent of salary, we can show this saving as a cash figure. It will inevitably be found that this figure will far outweigh any possible increase in cost entailed by purchasing snap-apart sets. It will be of interest to the reader to try this with actual figures.

FORMS CONSTRUCTION

It may now be advantageous to start discussing the relative merits and limitations of the various types of form construction before proceeding to the area of form design.

Carbon-Interleaved Cut Sets (*Glued at Head*)

If interleaved with one-time carbon paper, this is the cheapest, but most primitive, and therefore least efficient, type of form construction.

The reason for this construction is purely for ease of manufacture. In this type of flat-bed printing process the printing type may be set two-up, four-up, or more. If four-up, then each sheet of paper will contain four images, usually two pairs foot-to-foot. This not only cuts down the press time to a quarter, but it also allows the carbon interleaving to be reduced to one quarter of the time required if printed single-sheet. Naturally, on large-quantity work this is quite desirable from a printing point of view. Glueing on two parallel edges is then done on piles of sets with a brush, and when dry the full sheets are then cut down into four single sets. With special glues, separating between sets is no longer a problem.

These, then, are the advantages.

While the carbon paper has been inserted for the user and there is now no need to insert and jog by hand, the efficiency, however, stops there.

Because of the method of construction, the carbons are now the same length as the paper parts, so there is no facility for quick removal of the carbons when separating the set. Each part and carbon must be laboriously separated one by one—a time-wasting and costly operation. Sometimes the carbon is not even glued—but it still must be removed sheet by sheet.

It should be borne in mind that the foregoing remarks concerning one-time carbon interleaved sets refer to the flat-bed printing process. With rotary forms-printing equipment the interleaving problem is considerably reduced and, of course, carbon-removal features can be easily incorporated into the sets, thus reducing some of the advantages of the more expensive self-copying papers.

Self-Copying Papers

To eliminate the time-wasting carbon-removing operation, an alternative for such types of forms would be to print the forms or sets on self-copying stock, which requires no interleaving of carbon papers. Because of the edge-glueing, however, each sheet must still be detached one by one.

Self-copying papers also have some undesirable features, such as the fact that they may require careful handling in files, as some of them always retain their self-copying capabilities and so are easily marked at all times. Others lack body and can create problems in certain types of files. Dubious writing or printing surfaces and lack of variety of base stock, together with difficulty in copying from their image with certain duplicating or photocopying equipment, are some other problems which should be considered when contemplating such papers. Their cost may also be another factor which should be taken into account.

Their great advantage lies in time-saving in production of the forms, particularly in flat-sheet printing, by eliminating the need to collate with one-time carbons. Furthermore, they resolve the problem of having to dispose of the one-time carbons after separating the sets.

Another point which can be of importance is in an area where security has to be considered. With self-copying papers, of course, no tell-tale carbon paper is discarded—and a carbon can usually be read as easily as the copy itself. Certainly a point to remember in security circumstances.

In fact, the decision to use either self-copying paper or one-time carbon interleaved sets must be decided upon entirely by the particular circumstances of an application.

Pull-Apart or Snap-Out Sets

This is a much more efficient form, whether using carbon-interleaved or self-copying papers.

In this method of construction, a perforated stub, of not less than $\frac{5}{8}$ in (16 mm) depth to allow for fingergrip, should be made. All paper parts will be perforated by easy-tear perforations—usually four cuts to the inch, although this will be governed by the number of parts and the type and weight of paper parts. No perforations are required in the carbon, which will remain fast to the stub. The carbon should also be not less than $\frac{5}{8}$ in short of the paper parts. This, of course, means that all 'writing' areas must be clear of shortened carbons. See Illustration 8.

Illustration 8. Stub depth and short carbons

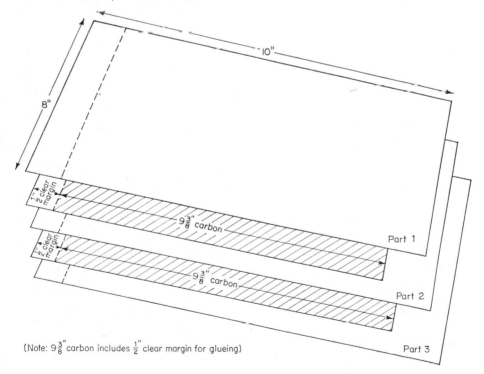

(Note: $9\frac{3}{8}$" carbon includes $\frac{1}{2}$" clear margin for glueing)

By holding the stub with the forefinger and thumb of one hand, and by gripping the clear area at a diametrically opposite point of the form by forefinger and thumb of the other hand, and then applying a steady pulling motion, the form will separate, leaving all the paper parts in one hand, while the stub with all the carbons will come away together in the other hand.

There is a technique about this which is well worth understanding. The term 'snap-apart', although commonly used, is a little misleading. If a jerky action is used there will always be a tendency for some of the paper parts to burst and tear incorrectly, thus causing mutilation of the part. An even pull is what is required for a clean tear.

The form should be held by the forefinger and thumb at the centre of the stub. Hold the stub in a horizontal position and allow the sheets to hang down as shown in the first illustration, 8(a).

As will be seen, this has the effect of allowing the sheets to 'fan', so that their bottom edges are a little staggered. Now, grip the 'fanned' edges firmly with the opposite hand, making sure the tips of the fingers are clear of the carbons, then raise the sheets to the horizontal position and it will be seen that the sheets are staggered, as illustrated at 8(a) and 8(b).

Pull–Apart Technique

Illustration 8(a). Fanning the set   Illustration 8(b). Horizontal for pull–apart

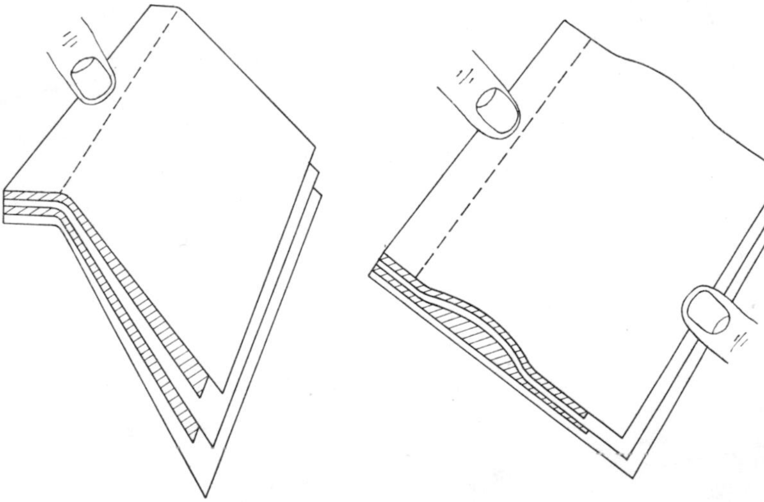

Thus, all the pulling pressure will be felt by each sheet sequentially—not simultaneously. They will now start to tear at the weakest point—which is, of course, the perforation.

Furthermore, if a little effort is made to ensure that the gripping points at each end are opposite each other, then the pressure will be applied initially on only about half an inch (10 mm) of the perforation. Once the perforation starts to tear, little further pressure is needed to complete the separation. In fact, by this fanning-and-pulling method each part is virtually torn separately, although only one movement is required.

A very large number of parts can be effectively separated by this method—and any problems in separation will be found to be caused by using a 'snapping' movement instead of a 'pull-apart' action.

Various Stub-Set Constructions

A number of variations of construction in stub sets can be implemented to secure increased efficiency in specific situations.

Extended Carbons: A simple time-saver which can be incorporated in a set lies in the use of a carbon which is longer than the paper parts—this extra length usually being an uncoated selvedge for cleanliness of handling. It is used where, say, a six-part combined acknowledgement-invoice-dispatch set is being initially typed up, and while the first four acknowledgement-invoice parts require to be separated the last two dispatch parts must remain fastened with a carbon for further common information to be added later.

In this case, presuming all paper parts to be of equal length, the fourth carbon would be $1\frac{1}{8}$ in (28 mm) longer than the other carbons and therefore $\frac{1}{2}$ in (12 mm) longer than the paper parts. The full extra length of $1\frac{1}{8}$ in can be uncoated, but at least the protruding half inch should be uncoated. This fourth carbon would also be perforated similarly to the paper parts. The set would be lightly glued between Parts 4 and 5, with the long carbon glued to the back of Part 4.

Now after typing, when the set requires to be split, the extended carbon indicates where the split should be, and by gripping at this fourth carbon the split can be easily made because of the light glueing. The carbon will, of course, tear at its perforation and come away with the back two-part portion, which is to remain still fastened together with the fifth carbon.

The extra care in manufacture is well rewarded by the ease with which the point of separation can be located and the split executed. Some forms may be designed with two separation locations.

Striped Carbons: With stub-sets, economical use can be made of the short carbons where, for special reasons, only part of the initial writing is required on one or more parts of the set. Similarly, striped patterns are easily manufactured if required for special purposes.

Such an example of striped carbons would be used, for instance, in a five-part request for quotation form, where the same specifications need be typed only

Illustration 9. Request For Quotation Form:— Using striped carbons. (Note. Sheet size – 8" x 11"; Carbon size – 8" x 10⅔")

once although addressed to four different suppliers. Form construction would be as shown in Illustration 9.

It will be seen that Part 1 will contain all the specifications and the names and addresses of the four suppliers to whom the request for quotation will be sent.

On the other hand, Part 2, while showing all the relevant specifications, will carry in Area (1) only one company name and address to whom the part should be sent—the other three names and addresses having been eliminated from the part by the arrangement of the carbon striping. Similarly, Parts 3, 4 and 5 will be sent to the second, third, and fourth suppliers—again with only their own names appearing in the respective Areas (2), (3) and (4), although identical specifications will have copied through on to each copy part.

If used in conjunction with window envelopes, then not only will the time required for typing envelopes be saved, but there will also be no chance of any copy going to the wrong supplier—and, it should be remembered, with only one typing.

Many other situations can arise where the use of such carbon stripes will be effective when circumstances require that certain areas of information should be suppressed in specific locations of particular parts of a business set.

Patterned Carbons: In addition to stripe-coating, carbons can also be patch- or spot-carbonized in an infinite variety of patterns to suit particular requirements. However, because patch- or spot-carbonizing is generally much more expensive than stripe-coating, it may be as well to define one from the other.

(1) *Parallel Stripe-Coated*: If the coated, or uncoated, stripes are of uniform width and run continuously from edge to edge in a parallel direction to each other, then the carbon is stripe-coated. See Illustration 10.

In this type of carbon the stripes always run the way of the paper web; that is, in the direction that the reel runs. There are few problems here, either in sheet-work or in reel-work.

Illustration 10. Parallel stripe-coated carbons. (Note: Carbon face down)

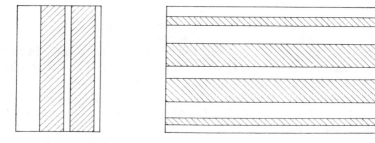

Illustration 11. Spot- or patch-coated carbons. (Note: Carbon face down)

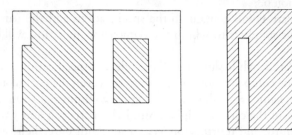

Any one, or all, of the above features would constitute patch-coating.

In reel-work, however, if the stripe runs across the width of the web, that is at right-angles to the length of the reel of paper, then this would be a patch-coated carbon.

(2) *Patch- or Spot-Carbonized:* If *any* stripes or areas stop short of one edge, are not uniform in their whole width, run at right angles to each other, or run across the web in reel-work, then the carbon is patch-coated. See Illustration 11.

Patch-coated carbons are used for the same purposes as stripe coatings, but are very much more expensive—though, if necessary because of the application, the extra expenditure may be well worth while for the efficient functioning of the procedure. However, before becoming involved in patch-carbonizing, take a long look at the design or layout of the form to see if re-design can eliminate the necessity for this device.

If circumstances demand patch-coating, then make absolutely sure that complete and precise measurements are given to the carbon manufacturer. This is best done by means of an accurate diagram indicating all measurements of both carbonized and uncoated areas.

It is vital that any carbon diagram MUST indicate clearly whether the pattern should be looked at as 'carbon face up' or 'carbon face down'. If this point is not made quite clear, there is a strong possibility that the pattern, in relation to other margins or edges, could be manufactured the wrong way round. In reel-work the unwind direction, and whether being unwound from the top or bottom of the reel, must also be clearly indicated.

Coloured One-Time Carbons

It is also as well to keep in mind that one-time carbons can come in many different colours such as blue, red, yellow, or green, and others if required. They can be used for many purposes.

For example, if coloured printing stock for some reason is not desirable in a set, then a coloured carbon can be used to identify a part, or parts, requiring particular attention or handling.

Blue: many people feel that a blue impression provides a sharper and stronger contrast than black, especially on coloured papers in certain tints of pink, green or yellow.

Red: Red is traditional for credit notes, and in many cases a considerable saving in printing costs can be realized if it is permissible to substitute red carbons for red printing. By a few minor type changes it is frequently found that an invoice form can be made acceptable as a credit note and run at the same time on the press and in the same colour of ink, thus eliminating a costly press wash-up for colour. Red carbons then provide the main distinguishing feature of one form from the other.

Yellow: The principal use of a yellow carbon is to provide a high degree of opacity on the underside of a translucent paper to back up a black image on the face for the photographic reproductive process in certain types of copying systems. Yellow is usually the top side of a double-sided carbon, the underside being a regular black.

Green: Green and other less usual colours, apart from their use for identification, are called for because of their 'prestige' value, in much the same way as special papers and ink tints are demanded.

The uses to which coloured carbons can be put are varied, and by a little ingenuity and thoughtful application some problems might be overcome by the use of coloured carbons.

Making Erasures on Stub Sets

One problem which occasionally arises concerns the difficulty of making erasures and subsequent corrections on the copy parts of stub-glued sets, if these errors or changes are being made during the typing operation.

There are, however, at least two possibilities of resolving this problem, which will arise with glued-at-head sets. Both of these solutions avoid the need to remove the set from the typewriter, thus eliminating the subsequent difficulty of realigning, both vertically and horizontally, when re-inserting the form after the erasures in order to type in the corrections and to complete the writing of the form.

To overcome this problem the sets could be constructed as follows:

Vertically Perforated Stubs: One way to allow erasures and corrections to be made on copy parts with stub-at-head sets is to perforate the stub vertically in two places, say, $1\frac{1}{2}$ in to 2 in (40–50 mm) apart at the centre of the stub. In this method of construction not only are the paper parts perforated along the full length of the stub, but the carbons must also be perforated to tear horizontally. See Illustration 12.

Illustration 12. Vertically perforated stub

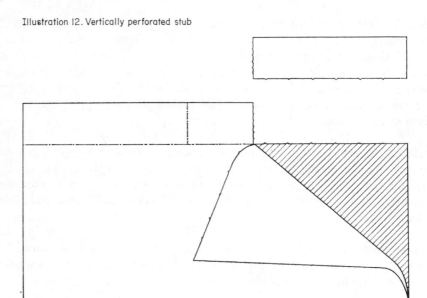

Thus, if an error is made on the left-hand side of the form, then the stub is torn down the left-hand vertical perforation and along the stub perforation to the left-hand edge. Access is now available to this side of the set for erasures, etc., while the parts and carbons are still securely held in alignment.

Similar action on the right-hand side of the stub would apply if the error or change occurred on the right-hand side of the form.

Even if both sides of the stubs are removed, the carbons will still remain attached to the remaining portion of the stub until the time arises for separating the set. The carbons, of course, being $\frac{5}{8}$ in (16 mm) shorter than the paper parts, will still be removed in one movement by means of the stub.

Bottom Stubs: The second solution, which is probably the simplest although perhaps not the most obvious, is to ensure that the stub is at the foot of the set rather than at the head, which is the most common construction.

It should be apparent that if the stub is at the foot of the set then the top edges will always be free to allow access for any erasures on the copy parts without removing the set at all, and this construction would appear to be the simplest way to overcome the problem of making corrections on glued sets.

Contrary to some opinions, there should be little difficulty in feeding the loose end of the set into a typewriter, unless the set is badly handled. The parts and carbons are fastened together to ensure that they do lie secured and flat. If there is any tendency for the parts and carbons to 'fan' during the initial stage of insertion, this can be quickly rectified when the pressure is taken off the set and the platen for squaring up the set in correct alignment and position for typing.

Only if long and short parts are embodied in a set, and then only if the top or bottom parts are short, is there likely to be serious trouble with a bottom stub—in which case a stub-at-head construction may be essential.

From an economical point of view, stub-at-foot construction can sometimes be found to be additionally attractive by offering a way of making a saving in carbon cost. Such a saving can be effected because most stationery will have anything from $1\frac{1}{2}$ in to 2 in (40–50 mm) of space to allow for company name, address, telephone number, etc., and as a result this space is denied for writing at all. At best only a single date-line will be involved. A further $\frac{5}{8}$ in (16 mm) should be left clear at the foot for a fingergrip on the stub to clear the carbons when separating the set. It is possible, therefore, to reduce the carbon size by taking advantage of the stub-at-foot construction. See Illustrations 13 and 13(a).

It will now be seen that the carbons in the stub-at-foot construction of Illustration 13(a) need only be an economical $8\frac{3}{8}$ in (210 mm) deep—instead of $10\frac{3}{8}$ in (260 mm) deep as in the stub-at-head construction shown in Illustration 13.

Continuous Forms

There are three main classes of continous forms: (1) for use in autographic register machines; (2) for use in typewriters, desk-model accounting machines, addressing machines, teleprinter machines, etc.; and (3) for use in tab-card tabulators or computer-output printers.

1. Autographic Register Forms

Register forms can, of course, be manufactured from one of many self-copying papers. In which case a simpler register machine than would normally be required may be adequate—and the succeeding remarks concerning carbon sheets and rolls will not apply. The main disadvantage of such papers may be that they will retain their self-copying properties into files. Such forms will also usually cost more, and this will be a continuing expense.

Hand-written register forms are normally manufactured without carbon-interleaving, the carbons being held within the machine either in sheet form or in rolls (two, three, or four-ply as required by the number of parts in the set). Generally, portable register models use carbon sheets. Counter-top models

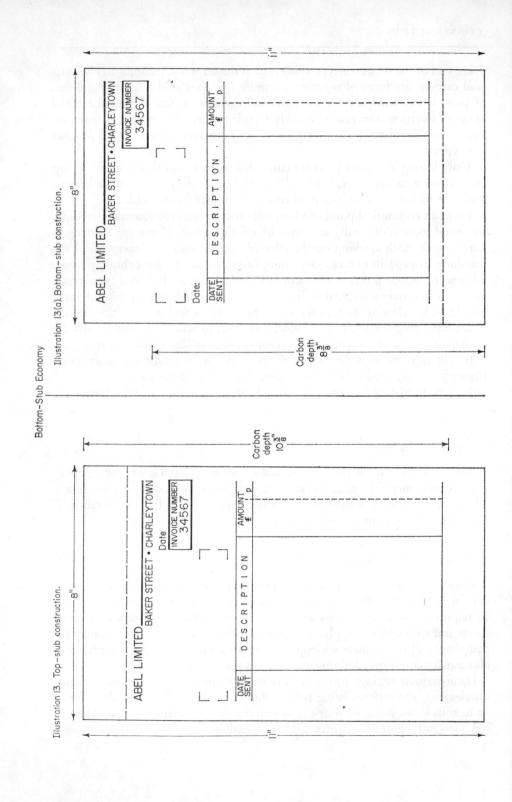

Bottom-Stub Economy

Illustration 13(a). Bottom-stub construction.

ABEL LIMITED
BAKER STREET • CHARLEYTOWN

INVOICE NUMBER
34567

Date:

DESCRIPTION

DATE
SENT

AMOUNT
£   p

Carbon
depth
8 3/8"

Illustration 13. Top-stub construction.

ABEL LIMITED
BAKER STREET • CHARLEYTOWN
Date

INVOICE NUMBER
34567

DESCRIPTION

DATE
SENT

AMOUNT
£   p

Carbon
depth
10 3/8"

will usually require carbon rolls, because of the larger forms-pack capacity of these bigger machines.

Some counter-top register models can have a self-advancing carbon device which provides a more even and economical use of the carbon while ensuring that fresh carbon is always being advanced for cleaner and sharper impressions at all times.

There are two main types of autographic register machines—friction-fed and pinwheel-fed, and it is obvious that where part-to-part registration is of little or no consequence then the friction-type register machine will perform adequately. Nevertheless, it is not difficult to appreciate that multiple-part sets of three or four parts must fan out when friction is applied only to the top and bottom parts, and this will be aggravated when the pack is folded in the zig-zag manner of continuous forms.

If, on the other hand, registration of vertical and horizontal ruling is required to ensure accurate part-to-part copy-through, then the pinwheel type of autographic register must warrant close consideration.

Exact part-to-part registration can be expected with pinwheel feed. This is, of course, because no friction is applied at all, the parts advancing solely by the pins engaging in the pinholes in the paper parts. The sheets, therefore, are automatically aligned with each other by means of the pins pressing against the top edge of the pinholes which are evenly and precisely spaced in the paper parts.

Again the choice of equipment must be entirely governed by the particular circumstances pertaining at that time.

It is also worth while keeping in mind that many variations in form construction can be incorporated into an autographic register application.

Variations on Register Forms Construction: In most register applications, for example, it is desirable that each set should be separated into single parts immediately it is ejected from the forms dispenser. However, there are circumstances where it may be convenient with, say, a four-part register set to have one section of two parts ejected as a fastened set with a one-time carbon between these parts to facilitate the addition of further data at a different location.

Such a form might be devised for a parts requisition procedure for a company who have a particularly large and complex parts store, such as will be found in the automotive or electronics industries.

It is certain that this would involve, say, a four-part set in counter-top models of autographic register machines. In this application the requisitioner would probably give a verbal description of the required part, sufficient to allow identification from a parts catalogue. This information would be written down on a consecutively numbered set, and the form ejected.

Part 4 would probably re-fold into a locked compartment, thus providing

E

a controlled check of each order written up each day in an unbroken continuous pack. Part 3 would be the requisitioner's copy, also numbered, which would be placed with the work order of the job for which the spare part is required.

Parts 1 and 2, with an interleaved one-time carbon, would be fastened together down one side, either with spot glueing or by means of wire stapling or crimplocking, and would be handled as a two-part set. Constant control would be maintained by means of the consecutive numbering.

This set would be sent to wherever the parts catalogues were located, and from the written description the correct catalogue part number, and perhaps the unit price, would be ascertained and written on to the two-part set. It is also likely that the stock room location number, and the shelf or bin number, would be obtained and posted to the set for ease of locating the part.

At this point the two-part set would be snapped apart, or otherwise separated, with Part 2 going to the Stores Department so that the order can be executed; while Part 1, after careful cross-checking, would proceed to the Accounts Department where the price extensions would be made. The final charge would then be allocated to the correct account or job number.

The above procedure is described to indicate the versatility that can be introduced into the construction of even an autographic register application to increase efficiency, ensure security and control by numerical checks, and to reduce or eliminate the needless copying of information. The manufacturers of autographic register equipment are always anxious to advise on the possible uses of their machines, and such advice should always be sought when contemplating a major change in such areas, as time-saving applications or construction can often be suggested.

2. *Continuous Typewriter Forms*

This type of construction can also be processed over accounting machines, addressing machines, etc.

Again, many factors govern the ultimate design, and it is only when *all* the circumstances are known and evaluated is it possible to decide on the most efficient construction of the form suitable to the particular situation. To start designing a form on a basis of presumed routines, 'hunches', and half-truths is virtually the formula for 'instant inefficiency'.

Substantiated facts are the only basis for form design; and when such facts are not available then intelligent deductions, based on known factors, should be thoroughly discussed with the personnel involved before incorporating changes into a design.

The day of the unquestioned 'super-expert' in this field is, thankfully, on its way out. It is to be hoped that consultation, co-operation, and common sense will be allowed to show the way to real efficiency.

As with register forms, there are two types of feeding, i.e. friction and pinwheel feed.

Friction-Fed Continuous Forms: Friction-fed forms are again less efficient and effective than the pinwheel type, mainly because the form must feed round the small circumference of the platen of a typewriter or accounting machine, and are thus prone to poor part-to-part registration and uneven advancement due to slipping.

The problem of part-to-part registration is much more serious in friction-feeding on typewriters than is the case with autographic registers. The tendency for the parts to 'fan' when going sharply round the platen is greatly exaggerated because friction is applied at precisely the point where the 'fanning' starts.

To combat this effect on sets, whether carbonless or interleaved with one-time carbon, most of this type of continous form have some method of fastening or locking the parts of each set. These methods range from crimplocking or wire-stapling at one side or centre of the set, to side-glueing one edge in order to counter the fanning effect.

It is as well to be aware, however, that this immediately creates two further problems: (1) since the set is now locked, a means must be provided to remove the carbons quickly, or to separate the parts if not carbon-interleaved; and (2), any side-fastening will mean that one side of the set will be thicker than the rest of the set and, therefore, with friction-feed the form will tend to run off the horizontal line while going through a machine.

This latter effect will be more pronounced in relation to any increase in the number of parts of a set, and the situation should be carefully considered when deciding on which type of manufacture to employ.

Fastenings: To facilitate friction feeding of typewriter forms there are at least five possibilities for locking the parts and carbons together to combat the fanning problem. Each method of fastening has its own advantage and dis-advantages—but it should also be remembered that a feature which is a handi-cap in one application may provide a desirable advantage in another procedure. For this reason it is important to understand each method of fastening. See Illustration 14.

(a) Glued Side-Stubs: This is a common method of fastening continuous forms where each set will be torn off and handled individually, and is one which causes little difficulty in manufacture with rotary equipment. It provides prob-ably the most secure fastening as well as an easy snap-apart, or pull-apart, action for effective separation of parts and removal of carbons by one simple movement, similar to any other pull-apart set.

Because of the successive layers of glue down one edge between the parts,

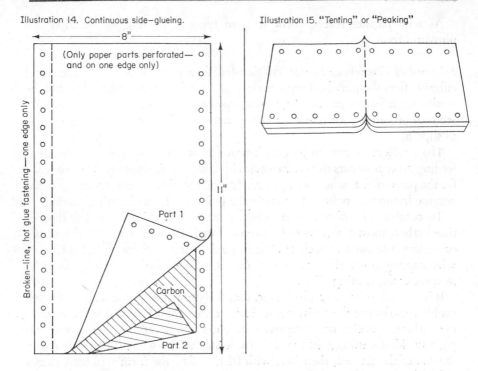

Illustration 14. Continuous side–glueing.   Illustration 15. "Tenting" or "Peaking"

however, this side becomes thicker than the rest of the set and so, if friction-fed, aggravates the problem of feeding evenly around the platen of the typewriter or the accounting machine.

It is advisable to use a broken-line or spot-patterned glueing procedure, and to use a hot glue (quick-setting glue).

If solid-line glueing is used in the manufacture of sets, then there is a real danger of 'tenting' on the fold edges. See Illustration 15.

The effect of 'tenting' is caused, usually with a solid-line glueing technique, by a slow-setting glue solidifying when the pack is zig-zag folded. Not only are the parts thus glued permanently out of alignment, because of the fanning due to the fold, but also a small brittle peak develops at each cross-fold which can cause jamming under guides when the form is being fed through a machine. Furthermore, when the set is being fed under the guide-pins the brittle 'tent' or peak may split and start to tear along the horizontal and sometimes the vertical perforations, causing frequent jams when the form is machine written.

As suggested, broken-line glueing with a hot, or quick-setting glue offers the possibility of fewest problems from 'tenting'.

(b) *Wire-Stapling One Side:* This is similar to a crimplocked construction, but the fastening of usually two wires per depth is more secure though also much

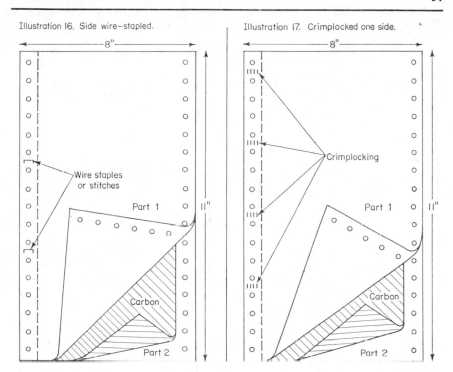

Illustration 16. Side wire–stapled.   Illustration 17. Crimplocked one side.

more expensive, as such stapling usually calls for a further operation in manu-facture. See Illustration 16.

It does not 'bulk' any more than crimping, but there is a slight danger that a staple could come out and cause damage by falling into the machine—though this is a possibility rather than a probability.

(c) *Crimplocked Side-Stub:* Crimping allows for a more even feed through the machine because there is less build-up on the side. There are also fewer problems in production with modern rotary equipment. Nor are there any problems relating to 'tenting'.

The main disadvantage of this method of fastening is that it does not hold parts and carbons too securely, and tearing apart is not so easy because there is no rigid stub to pull against. Crimping will not stand too much handling. See Illustration 17.

(d) *Corner Wire-Stapling:* In this method of fastening the paper parts must be angle-perforated at the top left as indicated in Illustration 18. The carbon paper must also be processed to have a slash at the bottom right, which should run down to join the bottom perforation at about one inch from the right-hand edge. Note that the perforation stops at this slash, thus, when tearing off,

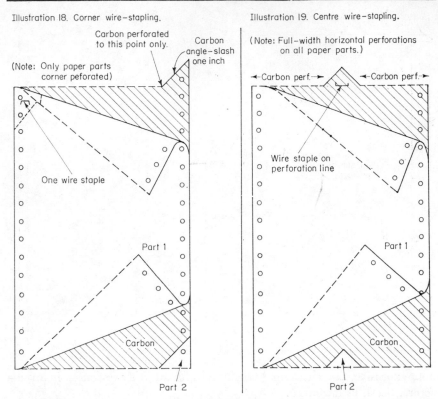

Illustration 18. Corner wire-stapling.

Illustration 19. Centre wire-stapling.

allowing a protruding tab at the top and a clear space for finger-grip at the foot. A pull-apart action will now separate the parts and extract the carbons. There is no need for a typist to handle actual carbon at all in this type of construction.

This is quite an effective construction if properly manufactured, but care must be taken to ensure that the perforations and slashes stop where indicated. It is vital that the correct strength of perforations for both paper and carbons is obtained, otherwise clear gripping areas will not be left where necessary for the removal of carbons and the separation of parts. It should also be noted, when tearing one set off from the others, that the tear must be started at the left edge, or the same side as the staple, to allow the carbon slash at the right end to function properly. See Illustration 18.

(e) *Centre Wire-Stapling:* This is similar in principle to the corner-stapled sets. This time the paper parts need no special perforations; only the carbons will require to have a centre vee-tab cut or perforation which, on tearing, would leave a clear space at the bottom of the set and an extended vee-tab of carbons at the top, for removing the carbons with one movement. Unfortunately, in this method the carbons themselves must be handled, which is an undesirable feature.

If the staple is positioned right on the perforation on the paper parts, then the staple will come away with the carbons for easy disposal. Illustration 19.

This method of stapling exactly on the perforation has the further advantage in that one staple will prevent fanning in both adjacent sets. Because of this, only one staple is required every two sets—on the out-fold perforation only.

3. *Marginally Punched Continuous Forms*

As was mentioned in connection with marginally punched and sprocket-fed autographic register forms, this is the ideal way to feed continuous forms because automatic part-to-part registration is ensured by the very method of pinwheel feeding. In a typing operation complete control is also assured, whether in moving the form forward or backward when accurately positioning for error corrections.

With typewriting and accounting machine operations no locking of any description is required for feeding or registration purposes with sprocket feeding. It must be clearly recognized that in this type of operation a locked form would be called for only because of a further handling operation at a later stage in the procedure.

Similarly, it must be realized that computer forms are fastened only because of the extremely high speeds at which the line-printers operate. This, allied to their very high running costs, makes it absolutely vital that stoppages for any reason whatever must be either eliminated or reduced to the absolute minimum. Therefore, the mere possibility of creeping carbons causing jams must be prevented—and, as a result, the trend now is to crimplock all computer forms. In these circumstances the locking of these forms is quite understandable and is recommended—providing some reasonable thought is given to the circumstances, and that fastening is not simply automatically specified.

This point is emphasized, because the very act of fastening a set for one reason or another immediately presents the problem of unlocking the set after the print-out or typing operation. There are, of course, many ways of locking and unlocking multiple-part sets, depending upon the circumstances surrounding the particular procedure. It must be obvious, however, that if there is no need to fasten a set in the first place then the problem of unlocking will not arise— and there will be one less problem to cope with.

With forms which are used in high-speed computer systems or tabulator operations, and where a great number of forms are being run off at a time, then the fastenings will more than likely be removed by slicing off the whole of the edges containing the fastenings by means of slitters, either when going through power-driven de-collators or forms bursters. In these circumstances the fastening-removal does not present too much of a problem and any delay can be reduced to a minium.

The disadvantages of locking forms become more apparent in operations involving relatively low volumes of forms, where the mechanical means of removing the fastening is denied because of the inconvenience of setting-up such equipment.

If the removal of the fastening must be done manually, as is usually the case in typewriter operations using continuous forms, then consideration must be given to whether fastening provides an advantage—or otherwise. Unless care and thought is given both to the design and to the construction of such forms, a high degree of inefficiency, causing undesirable waste of time, can be incurred by fastening a form when there is no need to do so, or by not anticipating a quick means of unlocking the form.

Since the extremely high speeds common to modern computer-output printers cannot be expected from typewriter operations—even those actuated and controlled by tape or punched cards—there is, generally, no real need to fasten together carbons and parts. Indeed, with pinwheel-platen feed there are good reasons why the sets should not be locked at all.

Pinwheel-Platen Feeding: To obtain the greatest advantages from pinwheel-platen feed on such as a typewriter, the parts and carbons must be entirely free and unfastened. Of course, no friction is now required for feeding. On the contrary, any friction now will only have an adverse effect on the feeding of the form. In fact, if there is any suggestion of continuous forms not feeding properly with pinwheel-platen feed, the very first fault to look for would be pressure from the typewriter platen. Friction must be taken right off.

It is important that these forms should be quite free to be gently jogged into exact alignment, vertically and horizontally, by means of the pins on the pinwheel pressing against the top inside edges of the pinholes in both paper parts and carbons as each line is typed and then advanced to the next writing line.

Because the space remains constant between the pins, and the distance across from one pinhole to the other is also fixed, then the location of any character or digit can be precisely re-located for any purpose whatever—even after the set has been removed from the machine and then re-inserted.

To ensure absolute accuracy in a re-typing operation, however, the form must be rewound back a few lines before the point at which the re-typing is required. The form will then be advanced again to the correct position and the re-typing can be performed accurately.

This procedure is required because the pinholes in the forms are slightly larger than the pins in order that there should be no jamming when feeding. However, this means that there would be a slight variation in line location between feeding a form forward and feeding it backwards. This problem is overcome by backing to some lines before the re-typing point and then advancing in the usual way, when extremely accurate re-working can be done which will scarcely be detectable.

Without any doubt, pinwheel-platen feed provides the most accurate method for a re-working where corrections or changes need to be neatly and quickly done. A further advantage of pinwheel-platen feed is that full control is exercised at precisely the point where it is needed—that is, at the writing-line position.

The foregoing remarks refer to pinwheel-platen feed and not to tractor feed, because the tractor feed, while using pins and pinholes, does not usually permit the form to be backed around the platen. In the case of tractor feed, the form would require to be lifted off the pins, backed by hand, and then re-positioned on the pins and re-wound forward to the position, when the final stages would be the same as for pinwheel-platen.

Left unfastened, the continuous typewriter form is a simple and accurate form and, if properly designed, the most easily handled of all interleaved forms. The separation of parts and removal of carbons presents fewer difficulties than any other type of form. This is regardless of whether large volumes are being used in daily runs, or where more moderate quantities are being processed and then torn off singly or in small batches according to the requirements of the procedure.

If always used in large quantities on each run it is probable that no special processing, apart from marginal punching, need be done to the carbons since they will more than likely be removed, after print-out, by means of a decollator or separator. Because of the complete freedom from locking or fastening, the very simple gravity separators behind the typewriter can be used. These will separate the parts from each other and re-fold them separately into individual packs, while allowing the carbons to be fed to waste. Bursting of these individual packs can now be done, either manually or by means of forms-bursting or guillotine equipment.

Should the operation call for small batches to be typed up and torn off the pack separately it is most likely that the carbons will require to be removed by hand. In this case, the construction of the form must include the means for 'whisking' out the carbons from the parts in one movement.

This can be done very effectively by angle-slashing the carbon from edge to cross-perforation at bottom left (or bottom right), or perhaps by a centre vee-slash as previously described under continous forms fastenings. Any of these constructions will leave protruding carbon tabs at the top of the set, with a corresponding clear space at the foot to permit a finger-grip on the paper parts. Since no fastening device has been employed the carbons are thus simply removed with very little effort.

While both side-tabs or centre-tabs do a similar job, preference is usually shown for the side-tab construction, unless the typographical layout of the form's design dictates otherwise. Naturally, the layout of the form must be considered before any decision is made with regard to construction.

All things being equal, however, there are fairly obvious reasons which favour side-tabs to centre-tabs. The first is that the side-slash is simpler to manufacture, since only one cut is required. Second, since sprocket feeding is involved, an uncoated selvedge down the length of the forms will allow for a non-carbonized area for clean handling when gripping for extraction.

Finally, it is much more certain that the perforation will be ready to tear right across the form in one steady progression, before meeting the slash in the side-tab construction. With centre-tabs, the form will tear along the perforation, then meet the centre slashes before starting to tear again along the second half of the perforation.

Whichever method is used to provide tabs and finger-grip, it is much more simple and effective in a loose form than in a fastened form.

Computer and Tabulator Forms: As has already been mentioned, because of the high speed and volume of sets which are required in systems using such equipment, it is the rule rather than the exception, particularly in computer-printer applications, that sets are fastened for running. However, once again it is advisable to consider whether or not fastening in a set is really required. Tabulator printing speeds are very much lower than those for most computer-output printers, and sets for such tabulators are much more easily processed after print-out if they are not fastened. Once again, if not fastened, their separation after print-out can be done quite effectively by means of simple gravity separators. If any form of fastening is used then power de-collators, etc., are usually called for.

Wire-staple fastening can be used on some types of set, although data-processing equipment manufacturers advise against this method of fastening and usually recommend crimplocking as an alternative. Staples provide a more secure fastening than crimping when extensive handling after print-out is called for, but they involve a more expensive method of manufacture.

In the area of computers and tabulators there is a great usage of stock listing forms, and while these can be obtained unfastened they are generally crimp-locked for high speed feeding.

The call for ever-higher speed in print-out equipment has induced a call for heavier paper stocks to be used, as they feed more easily and cause less trouble when running. It should also be remembered that heavier stocks make clear and sharp copies more difficult to obtain and very often the important need to procure a better grade of carbon paper is either overlooked altogether or ignored because of supposed economies. Whatever savings are shown in an estimate or cost sheet, they are seldom justified if resultant poor copies are obtained on the form.

Such 'economies' should be treated for what they are—the mark of confused and dangerous thinking. It is much better to have slightly more expensive carbon and a better-than-required copy than a cheaper carbon which can only supply a less-than-satisfactory impression.

The construction and design of computer and tabulator sets must be examined even more carefully than usual before finalizing because of the high hourly cost which is involved in such systems, and the resultant heavy cost factor which will accrue if inefficiencies are allowed to creep in. Because of the extremely high rate of forms-processing in modern output printers the cost of an error, or an inefficiency, is compounded to an alarming degree in this situation.

Whilst it is true that most people realize the benefits which can be obtained from the efficient utilization of a computer system, despite the apparent high cost, not everyone appreciates that the converse is also true. An inefficient application, for example by poor form construction, can either incur pro-hibitive costs in relation to value obtained or, at best, can severely restrict the possible benefits from the operation.

It is, therefore, quite important that the full potential of a form, both in design and construction, should be completely understood in order that 'func-tional ability' will be incorporated into the form to the highest possible degree.

It will be realized that the observations made regarding typewriter continuous forms, with reference to unfastened or fastened sets, apply equally to computer and tabulator continuous sets, with a greater need for fastening on computer sets.

Extra Copy Singles

Very frequently overlooked when considering forms applications is the use to which an over-run of 'singles' can be put. This applies to stub-set as well as to continuous-set applications.

While the number of parts in most sets can be judged for normal usage there will almost certainly be occasions when extra copies will be required because of special circumstances. There is no reason at all why this kind of circumstance cannot be anticipated and be taken into account when the form, or a re-order of the form, is being put into production.

This is merely another way of enhancing and extending the 'functional ability' of a form by ensuring that the procedure has a little built-in flexibility which can allow for a slight divergence from the normal requirements of a routine. In fact, not to make such allowances is an indication of inefficiency in the procedure—which is precisely what should be avoided where possible.

When no singles are ordered with sets, then the only way to obtain extra copies is to strip down whole sets and use the parts as extras. In the first place, the parts and carbons will have been separated so this now means trying to handle makeshift extras. This is not always easy when dealing with stub sets, since the extra parts will now be $\frac{5}{8}$ in (16 mm) short of the full set and, consequently, could get out of alignment.

Secondly, since the extra copies will usually be required in white, any coloured parts will be useless as copy parts and a full set may be torn up to provide only one or two copies. If the sets are sequentially numbered, then they just cannot be used, and another substitute single must be found.

If, however, the need for extra copies is anticipated and allowed for at an early stage, then a small but adequate quantity can be ordered to be run with the full set. In this way a most advantageous price will be obtained even for a quite small quantity of singles, which should, of course, be exactly the same size as the full set, and have a one-time carbon glued to the perforated stub on the face if part of a glued-stub set.

Furthermore, not only can the singles be distinctively designated 'Copy' if so desired, but if the sets themselves are sequentially numbered with an alphabetical, or numerical, prefix then this can also be run on the singles and space left to type or mark in the appropriate number of the set for which the extra copy is being made.

When one or more extra copies are required of the document, then these prepared singles are simply lifted and placed behind the set and typed up without any further trouble, and the carbon can be removed in the same movement which separates the parts and carbons of the full glued-stub set.

If it is felt that a better copy would be obtained by inserting the singles into the set rather than at the back, then care should be taken to trim the stub of the singles so that it will rest against the glue line of the full set—say, one quarter of an inch short of the other parts.

In continuous sets it is similarly easy and economical, if anticipated in the early stages, to order singles to be over-run and have a carbon on the face and made up into convenient packs. Here again they can be specially designated with 'Copy' and have numbering prefixes printed on so that only the actual number need be added.

In operation, especially if used with sprocket-platen feed, these copy sheets can be either torn off singly from the pack, or the two packs can be merged to provide a set with an extra copy, as alignment will be precise, and of course the pack of singles can be removed at any time.

Also, a company which uses the same basic form in various locations, but requires a different number of parts for certain branches, can accomplish this by the expedient of adding copy singles as required.

There are, of course, many other circumstances where the device of adding interleaved singles can resolve probems or improve efficiency by reducing the duplication of effort in 'writing'. The most common application would be extra 'copy' parts for invoices, dispatch advices, or production instructions. Less obvious circumstances might be when providing extra copies, required on perhaps infrequent occasions, of data analyses of such things as periodic sales statistics, etc.

As will now be realized, the 'functional ability' of any form can be extended in many ways, and the mind should always be kept open for ideas which will enlarge still further the scope or effectiveness of the form.

More and more it will become apparent that the terms 'capacity' and 'functional ability' go far beyond mere size in a form.

The ability to resolve a problem in a forms application calls for not only a receptive and retentive mind with regard to ideas, but it also calls for an imaginative mental approach that will not deny consideration to an unusual or original suggestion.

Because of the variable factors, even in the same kind of company in the same industry, and because of the ceaseless demand for more and more up-to-the-minute information but with a different emphasis for each separate company, there is virtually an infinite permutation of design possibilities. Without any doubt 'standard body' forms must have their place in the scheme of things, but the need abounds for special designs and constructions, in order to attain the highest possible degree of efficiency under each individual set of circumstances.

As the need for some knowledge of the various types of forms was required, so the need for some knowledge of paper stocks which might be useful in certain circumstances is also of great value.

Special Papers

People dealing with forms can usually recognize the more common grades of stationery paper stocks, self-copying papers, at least some colours and grades of one-time carbons and the uses which can be made of them—and may probably have with some idea, too, of their limitations.

How many, however, take the time to think of the potentialities of less well-known papers such as transluscent stocks, gummed papers, etc? For example, duplicating masters might be incorporated into a set, so that the original 'writing' can provide a quick means of procuring further copies where circumstances demand them.

There is also a very misguided but widely held belief that multiple-part forms and duplicating systems are a substitute for each other. In fact, forms and duplicating systems are complementary to each other. It is always advisable, when contemplating the incorporation of a duplicating master into a set, to consult both the printer and the duplicating equipment manufacturers, who will in most cases co-operate closely with each other. By co-operation the greatest efficiency will result—to the mutual benefit of all concerned.

Combined Applications

Areas which are frequently overlooked, and in which a substantial efficiency can be introduced by means of properly designed business forms, are the ware-housing and dispatch departments. The responsibility and necessity of writing dispatch advice notes can be eliminated from these departments by incorporating such documents into, say, an invoice set to produce a combined invoice/shipping advice form, so that all the essential information will thus be copied on to the shipping documents at the original typing.

Information which is not required on certain parts would be eliminated by means of block-outs, cut-outs, cut-out carbons, stripe- or patch-coated carbons; or, in the case of certain self-copying papers, by de-sensitizing the areas which are not required to reproduce impressions.

(a) *Labelling or Package Marking:* Another area which calls for close investigation is in the packaging and labelling department, particularly in those businesses where each order comprises a considerable number of parcels, boxes, or packages. In these circumstances the task of hand-writing or typing the same information repetitively on twenty or thirty labels for each job is not only laborious but is also boring and, as a result, errors may creep in—which, if not actually ruinous, can be embarrassing and the cause of much waste of time.

There are a number of ways of solving the problem, among which would be the use of a typewriter controlled and activated by means of paper tape or punched or edge-punched cards, which would automatically type up the required number of continuous labels.

A simpler way might be to include a stencil label master as part of a set which contains the information required to appear on each package, whether this would be addressing information or simply identification of the contents of the package. Such stencilling systems supply a holder and inking attachment, which makes the marking of packages a very simple and fast operation. Furthermore, not only is time itself saved to a great degree, but the cost of the printing of labels may be either eliminated or at least reduced in many cases.

It should be worth mentioning that although the suggestion has been made that the labels might be dropped in favour of stencilling, it is important to realize that it should not be assumed that stencilling will *always* be favoured against labelling. It is merely suggested that in *certain circumstances* this might be so; but the very reverse might just as well be recommended in another set of circumstances.

It is very important to grasp the fact that circumstances will control not only a system but also the design and construction of a form.

While on the subject of labels, it should be borne in mind that the destination, or 'ship to', portion of at least one part of the shipping document can frequently be so perforated that, after typing, it can be torn out and used as a label by coating the back with gum. It is also possible to insert a label, as such, into a set either on gum-backed stock or on one of the self-adhesive papers.

With respect to this latter suggestion of the use of gum or self-adhesive paper, it is hoped that care will be taken to ensure that in this case printing is not being done by the lithographic process. Obviously the damping requirements of the lithographic process would play havoc with any such types of gummed stock.

Similarly, single gummed labels of the above type should never be considered for addressing by means of a copying master contained in a set—if the system is a wet process. Once again, the moisture in the system would render it impractical for addressing on to a gummed stock.

The labelling operation is one which frequently invites investigation because of the repetitive nature of the application and the desire to avoid or reduce a time-wasting task. This is as it should be, but make sure that fact-finding in the area is intensive and complete to the last point. Keep in mind, particularly, that surfaces such as waterproof wrapping papers and some plasticized surfaces are not always conducive to successful adhesion by ordinary means. Make sure that thorough tests are carried out in such projects before ordering stocks, by establishing that the label will in fact be able to adhere to the intended surface.

It may be felt that such considerations are quite obvious. Even so, for anyone who may not have thought too much about it, the warnings are worth repeating.

(b) *Pressure Labels:* If circumstances are against the use of moisture-activated adhesive stocks, do not overlook the possibility of using the pressure-adhesive type of label. These are usually carried on a plastic-wax-coated backing paper which protects the adhesive side while retaining the label. This type of label has many uses, because labels of any shape can be carried on the carrier backing which in turn can be marginally punched for sprocket feeding. Thus, although the bulkiness of this type of label may sometimes preclude the possibility of inclusion within a stub set, it could be fed from a separate continuous pack, along with the continuous set proper, when being written up on a sprocket-fed machine.

In a continuous-forms application the addition or removal of a separate pack of labels is a simple matter, and need not interfere too much with the normal working of such forms in, say, a typing operation.

(c) *Laundry Tag:* This is another type of stock which frequently finds its way into a set. This particular tag is usually impervious to the action of the washing and dry-cleaning agents used in laundry operations, as is the special printing ink also used. Because of the thickness and toughness of this stock, it is usual that the tag will be the last part of the set, and this will normally be satisfactory, providing the impression comes from the top sheet down.

If, however, the fact-finding discloses that data encoding equipment is being used which calls for positive plates, and the plate is applied to the back of the set so that the impression must come through the tag, then particular care should be taken. In these circumstances write-tests, using dummy sets, must be made quite early in the manufacturing process to make absolutely sure that correct weights and qualities of paper stock and carbons are being used in the set to guarantee satisfactory copy-through in this application.

Do not wait until the forms are ready and about to be put into use before establishing whether or not the impression is going to be acceptable—because if they are now found to be unacceptable at this point, then a first-class crisis is imminent, with little chance of a solution before real disruption is caused to the procedure.

(d) *Safety Papers:* This type of 'special' is widely used in cheque applications although it can, of course, come up in various other forms such as insurance certificates, guarantee forms, etc. In fact, safety papers may be used in any circumstance where security is involved, and where it is important that erasures or alterations are undesirable or, at least, where they must be easily identified.

The safety feature, of course, lies in the special pattern on the paper stock so that when an erasure is made by any means not only is the 'writing' removed, but so also is the safety pattern. This means that while characters could perhaps be unobtrusively replaced by other characters, it would be virtually impossible to replace the colour and design of the erased portion of the safety background pattern.

The same effect can be obtained by printing patterns in safety or fugitive inks on ordinary printing papers, and the decision to use one method or the other will, again, depend on circumstances and costs.

(e) *Tab-Card Stock:* This stock is appearing more and more frequently in multiple-part sets as the advantages of computerization, and electronic data-processing in general, become more widely recognized and implemented. There is an ever-increasing field for the set containing a 'tab' card which will, by one means or another, have information 'written' on it, and will subsequently have some or all of this data read, by human effort or by mechanical or electronic means, and then punched into the card itself.

The tab-card stock presents some problems in set manufacture because most equipment manufacturers specify that the grain of the card must run the long way, to minimize possible adverse effects of atmospheric changes. Furthermore, the surface of this card is very hard and well calendered, which is an essential requisite to ensure that the card will slide easily along in the various types of punching and sorting equipment which is part of any data-processing system, mechanical or electronic, which uses punched cards.

Because of the hardness of surface, which cannot be modified for the reasons just mentioned, particular care must be taken in the choice of carbon which will copy down on to the tab card. The card offers little or no absorption to any of the regular grades of wax carbons, and so the image simply sits on the surface of the card. Not only will the image smudge at the lightest touch, thus making reading more difficult, but the carbon-wax coating will also set-off on to any of the advancing-rollers with which it comes in contact throughout the data-processing system. This could result in successive cards being badly marked, as well as introducing the possibility of eventual jamming or slowing down of sensitive equipment by this accumulation of carbon deposit.

It is, therefore, absolutely essential that the carbon chosen must be capable of imparting a very dry image, which must also be of a uniform high-density black colour to ensure a fine, sharply defined image.

Maximum attention must be given to the choice of carbon for this application, and strict tests must be made to ensure that all requirements are met for optical reading and card processing. It cannot be over-emphasized how critical this factor will be in any optical character recognition system. It is essential to appreciate that only special O.C.R. (Optical Character Recognition) carbons should be considered, whether these are solvent coatings or the plastic-based pigment types of one-time carbons. It is, indeed, a false economy in this instance to settle for a cheap carbon—instead of the most effective one.

Optical Readers

There are many variations in optical readers, but for use with punched-card sets there are two main basic pieces of equipment involved: data recorders and optical readers or scanners. Data-imprinting machines, using embossed plastic or metal cards and fixed plates for non-variable information and wheel-mounted characters for variable information, are used for 'writing' the data on to the sets. There are also two main types of encoding systems 'languages': the simple bar-code, and the more versatile alpha-numeric O.C.R.-type fonts. The latter usually require a higher degree of character definition than the former.

Minimum tolerances vary between the different types of optical scanners or readers which handle either of these information systems. The bar-code scanners are usually relatively less critical than O.C.R. readers with regard to the quality of image necessary for acceptable recognition rates. However, even these more moderate specifications regarding combination of density of colour, clarity ot image, and dryness, are beyond the capabilities of regular one-time carbons— particularly with reference to problems related to 'smudge' and lack of cleanliness.

The more sophisticated O.C.R. font systems call for a much higher degree of efficiency in the provision of an image which will be acceptable to ensure a high rate of 'through-put' of cards being used with O.C.R. reader-card-punch equipment.

Cost of Rejection: Not only is there a high financial outlay in an optical recognition system, but there may also be little or no control, or even supervision, over the personnel and locations where the original data imprinting is done, whether this is a stock-room, a garage, or a large store or shop. It is, therefore, vital to the economic success of the installation and the application that the rejection rate of cards by the reader should be kept to the very minimum, despite adverse circumstances.

It should be realized that expensive equipment which will optically read and then punch the information into the same card at rates of upwards of 500 cards per minute could, because of poor impressions, have a rejection rate of between 5 and 15 per cent. This would mean that these rejected cards would then have to be read and key-punched by human effort—which is not only defeating the very principle of the automation of data-processing, but is also relatively very slow and expensive.

It means, furthermore, that a highly sophisticated and costly system may be wasting up to 15 per cent of its time in performing a completely useless task at a very high hourly rate. An expensive inefficiency.

If 15 per cent of the annual cost of the machine is calculated, and then to this figure is added the annual cost of processing the rejected cards by hand-punching, a very impressive figure, which is the true cost of the rejection rate, will be produced.

As this rejection rate can be considerably reduced by the use of the type of carbon most suitable for an O.C.R. system, the extra expense which would be involved for an acceptable carbon now becomes very reasonable, and even attractive, compared to the expense which is involved in a high rate of card rejection. Consideration of the efficiency factor may make any additional expense for a suitable carbon much more acceptable.

The above remarks will apply equally to optical page- or document-reading systems when carbon copies are being read.

Whichever optical reading system is used it should now be apparent that great care must be taken with the choice of carbon. The old 'anything-will-do' attitude will simply not do at all.

Tab-Card Set Construction

When considering tab-card sets for use in an optical reader-punch-card system, a few basic points should be kept in mind with regard to stocks to be used with the tab card.

Careful thought must be given to the sequence of parts and carbons within the set itself in accordance with the requirements of the reading and punching equipment and the type of data recording or imprinting equipment being used. It is also advisable, as previously mentioned, to take heed of the circumstances of the recording operation.

Once again, a fact-finding systems study will indicate the minimum number of parts required in a forms set to perform adequately the functions necessary for the system to operate efficiently. As always, however, there are limitations to the number of parts which can reasonably be expected to function adequately. This number will be dependent upon the type of equipment used, standard of quality of image demanded, weight and substance of stocks to be incorporated into the set, and many other factors.

It should be remembered that data-imprinting or recording equipment in tab-card operations is usually of the non-inking positive-plate type. This means that the plastic plate containing the impression image of the data will be placed on the base of the imprinter. The forms set will now be placed on top of the plates and imprinting discs in the machine, and pressure will be applied from the top—either by means of a lever action or by a pressure-roller action.

It will be realized, of course, that the construction of the set will be governed by the degree of sharpness of image required for reading purposes—whether by personnel, by mechanical means, or by optical character recognition equipment. Another circumstance which would have to be taken into account for construction would be whether negative encoding plates (set face down on plate) or positive encoding plates (set face up) are to be used.

Most tab-card sets are of the three-part type, using a translucent part, a medium weight (say 11 lb bank) part, a tab card, and two carbons—one of which is double-sided (or 'full'). Distribution of the parts would be: Part 1—retained by point of issue; Part 2—customer's copy; Part 3—to central data-processing system.

In this construction, the double-sided carbon lies between the translucent sheet (Part 1) and the bank sheet (Part 2), with a single-sided carbon (or 'semi-carbon') between Part 2 and the tab-card (Part 3).

The images are therefore reproduced by means of the double-sided carbon on to the underside of the translucent part, on to the face of the bank part by means of the underside of the double-sided carbon, and on to the face of the tab card by means of the second single-sided (optical character recognition) carbon, when the set is put into the imprinter and pressure is applied by lever or roller on to the set. See Illustration 20.

Illustration 20. Tab-card set—Positive image.

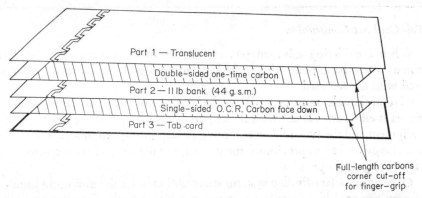

Part 1 — Translucent

Double-sided one-time carbon

Part 2 — 11 lb bank (44 g.s.m.)

Single-sided O.C.R. Carbon face down

Part 3 — Tab card

Full-length carbons
corner cut-off
for finger-grip

This is the method that would be employed to give a positive image if the cards are being read either by some optical methods or by personnel who would then key-punch the information into the same card. But great care is needed to ensure that the image on the tab-card is not soft and easily smudged, thereby causing many problems and much trouble.

It must also be realized that, if positive plates are used, the image may not be as sharp or as clear as it could be, since it has had to be pressed through the thick and tough tab-card before even reaching the copying agent, in this case the black one-time carbon. Nevertheless, in general, there will be no problem in securing an image which will be quite satisfactory for interpretation by human effort.

The quality of image is much more critical, however, if recognition is being carried out by optical reading equipment.

If a bar-code system is being used, then the three-part set construction previously described will be acceptable, presuming that the requirements relating to the carbons are met. Providing there is a reasonable and uniform depth of colour, and the image is dry, there should be few problems.

On the other hand, if an optical character recognition system is being operated, then, while it is probable that a three-part form might still be required, it may be advisable that the set construction should be rearranged. The quality of image may be required to be of a higher standard than that which was acceptable for bar-code reading.

If the optical reader can read a negative image, then the following set construction should be considered for positive plates.

To assist in effecting the necessary quality of image in processing on a data recorder machine, a rearrangement of the parts in the set could be undertaken in order that the image should not have to be impressed through the card itself.

In this construction two double-sided one-time/O.C.R. carbons should be used. This is because both sides of the tab-card should be imprinted—one side with a negative image which will be read by an optical reader, and the uppermost side with a positive image impressed for reading by human personnel when making changes or corrections, or when the card has been rejected for some fault. The O.C.R. side of both carbons will be against the card.

This construction would have a translucent sheet as Part 1, followed by a double-sided carbon with the one-time regular carbon side uppermost against the underside of the translucent sheet and the O.C.R. side underneath in contact with the tab-card which follows. Part 2 will be the tab-card, followed by the second double-sided one-time/O.C.R. carbon with the O.C.R. side uppermost against the underside of the tab-card. Finally, as Part 3, a paper stock which might be of a substance slightly heavier than usual to assist in collating with the card in the middle. See Illustration 20(*a*). As will be seen, the effect of this con-

Illustration 20(a). Tab-card set—Negative image.

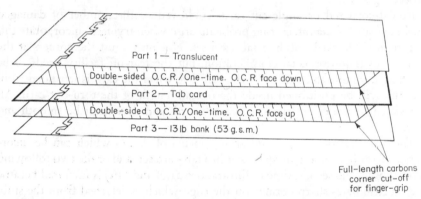

Part 1 — Translucent

Double-sided O.C.R./One-time. O.C.R. face down

Part 2 — Tab card

Double-sided O.C.R./One-time. O.C.R. face up

Part 3 — 13 lb bank (53 g.s.m.)

Full-length carbons
corner cut-off
for finger-grip

struction will be to produce a negative image on the underside of the tab card—but since the image need only come through a paper part and a carbon, it must be sharper and truer than would be the case if the image was coming through the tough card as in the first construction. Just remember that the reading equipment must be able to read negative images before using this construction.

When dealing with tab-card sets more attention than usual should be paid to materials and construction, to ensure that maximum through-put is maintained by the cards once they are introduced into the data-processing system. Since, as has already been mentioned, control is likely to be uneven or slack over the initial documentation and handling processes, some thought should be given to any areas which might protect the sets or the tab-cards once the sets have been split up into their individual parts.

While remaining within the set there is some protection for the tab-card, but once the set is split up then the card is initially at the mercy of people who are not card-conscious data-processing personnel. Shop assistants, garage attendants, spare-parts storemen, etc., are really much more concerned with carrying out their regular duties rather than with cosseting a piece of card, which to them may only be a half-understood nuisance in the first place. There must always be the constant possibility of careless handling damaging the card sufficiently to cause rejection by an optical or mechanical reader-punch unit.

As is reasonably well-known, folds in tab cards, or tears, or damaged edges and corners are the most usual causes of rejection. It may take some time to educate and convince the general public, as well as some employees, that much of the trouble which is encountered when dealing with folded or torn cards could be avoided by more care in handling the cards.

Something can be immediately done, however, to reduce the tendency to damage which is inherent in square-cornered cards. The right-angled corner is particularly accident-prone, and being bruised, bent, or dog-eared will be the fate of many of them—resulting in the possible rejection of them in a data-processing system.

Round-cornered or angle-cut cards could reduce the number of damaged cards, but special manufacturing problems arise when trying to incorporate this feature into the card within a tab-card set. Not only must the corners at the extremities require special consideration, but the tear-off facility needs to be carefully designed to ensure that the tufts left when the card is separated from the stub will be positioned inside the overall length of the torn-out card. All outside edges are critical factors in a tab card, and they must be smooth and true.

There are various shapes and arrangements of slashes which can be incorporated to allow for a snap-apart tear in a tab-card set, and of the two following types shown, the second type in Illustrations 21(b) and 21(c) is favoured because it even eliminates sharp corners on the edge which is detached from the stub. See Illustrations 21, 21(a), 21(b), and 21(c).

Whichever design of tear-off is decided upon, the tufts which are left after snapping apart must not protrude beyond the outside edge of the card, so the detached card must look something like that shown in Illustration 21(c).

If it is felt that rather a lot of attention has been paid to detail, it should be kept in mind that a tab-card set normally implies processing through very costly equipment. It also indicates that a high through-put of cards by this system will mean that a particularly high volume of relatively expensive tab-card sets is being contemplated to justify the use of a complex and high-cost card read-punch system. Therefore, inattention to detail could produce, or permit, very costly errors.

One of the more sobering aspects of multiple-part business forms is that if a mistake is allowed through production it is seldom that the forms can be used for any other purpose than that for which they were specifically designed. Errors usually result in a complete write-off of the whole run of forms. Not many companies can afford to indulge in mistakes of this magnitude for too long.

Details are very important. If any doubt exists, do not be afraid to seek and

Illustration 21. Tab card tear

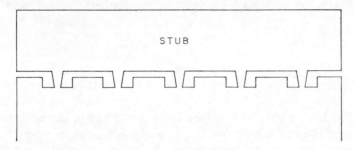

Illustration 21 (a). After separation from stub; recessed tear points

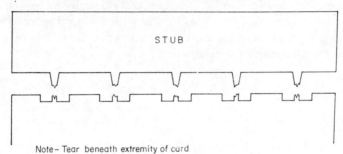

Note – Tear beneath extremity of card

Illustration 21(b). Preferred tear pattern

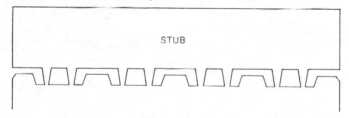

Illustration 21 (c). After separation; recessed tear points.

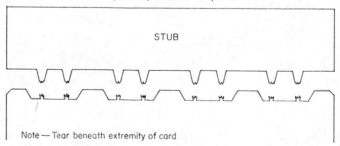

Note — Tear beneath extremity of card

consider advice from experts in that particular area. If the advice is conflicting, stop and consider carefully before proceeding further. Caution must be the key-note.

Section Conclusion

As will be realized, the purpose of this section has been primarily to direct attention to the importance of ensuring that consideration is always given to the three basic objectives of a business form or set; that is, ease of documentation, ease of information storage, and ease of information retrieval.

In suggesting how these objectives might best be achieved, it may be that digressions have been made into areas which may have been more the concern of the succeeding section. This latter section will primarily be concerned with guidance for typographical layout, as well as with a general approach to considering how the usefulness and capacity of a business form may be extended to provide maximum functional capacity.

3 DESIGN AND LAYOUT

The natural sequence of events has been followed from the origination of a multiple-part business form, that is, a fact-finding inquiry, and having decided exactly what information is required to appear on the form, and having also decided the number of parts required to achieve the full function of the document.

It now remains to be decided just how the type and type rules should be displayed to ensure maximum ease of documentation and information retrieval; and, furthermore, how the utmost efficiency and effectiveness can be obtained from the form by the judicious and imaginative use of such type and rules. In addition, perforations, consecutive numbering, stock and ink colours, special papers, aperture cuts, fastenings, and many other items and processes may require to be incorporated into the make-up of a business form to enhance its functional capacity.

It is not a straightforward matter to lay down anything remotely like a set of hard-and-fast rules to apply to a business form. As has been mentioned before, the varying requirements of business forms are virtually infinite in companies throughout the business world. Rather, an attitude of mind can be encouraged that will judge the forms on the basis of answers to questions such as the following.

Ten Points for Efficiency

Does the form allow maximum efficiency on the following points?

(1) Ease of documentation
(2) Information storage
(3) Information retrieval
(4) Readability
(5) Size and shape
(6) Number of functions performed
(7) Ease of handling in operation
(8) Aesthetic appeal
(9) Cost-relative-to-efficiency factor
(10) General functional ability.

Having suggested that affirmative answers to these questions will certainly give assurance of an efficient business form, it is not intended that they should be regarded as the only questions which should be asked. They do, nevertheless, go a considerable way along the correct road, and they are valuable as a basis for acquiring the correct attitude for approaching business forms.

What may now be emphasized is the need to utilize every facet of layout to ensure that maximum effectiveness is obtained throughout the design. It will be realized that the approach to forms design will vary, being dependent upon the method of 'writing' or documentation and many other circumstances and factors. Because of this, specific guides or laws are difficult to standardize.

Regardless of the difficulty of establishing hard-and-fast rules, however, it is possible to offer illustrations of action which can be taken in circumstances which are quite common and which arise frequently. Such illustrations may not only be useful in themselves, but may again encourage the true questing attitude of the business forms designer, who will always be looking for ways of extending the capacity and/or efficiency of a form, whether the circumstances happen to be commonplace or extraordinary.

Type Area

It is important to decide what will be the maximum limitations of the printed type area within the decided sheet size before starting to arrange the type and rules. Firstly, the 'writing' method must be taken into account; e.g. (1) hand-written; (2) plate or machine imprinted; (3) typewritten or accounting-machine processed; (4) processed in tabulator or computer-output printer.

As a general guide, it can be said that except in very specific circumstances type should never appear closer than an absolute minimum of $\frac{3}{8}$ in (9 mm) from any edge of the form, even a form without marginal holes. It is most advisable that margins of at least $\frac{1}{2}$ in (12 mm) be regarded as generally desirable. If a snap-out form, the finger-grip edge should, of course, have not less than $\frac{5}{8}$ in (16 mm) margin. Not many people have fingers which are sufficiently strong yet slim enough to separate forms comfortably with less than a $\frac{5}{8}$ in fingergrip to clear the shortened carbons.

Apart from the primary consideration of the aesthetic appeal of reasonable margins, there are many practical reasons why margins should not be less than $\frac{1}{2}$ in (12 mm). In flat-bed printing processes a clear margin should be left for the 'grippers' when feeding the sheet. Similarly, in rotary printing presses some reasonable space is required in the 'gutters' to allow for the securing of printing plates to the cylinders. Furthermore, slitting and perforating appliances require some room for being secured in order to perform their function.

In the vast majority of cases it will be quickly found that very little alteration of a form will be required to ensure that these minimum margins can be obtained. Almost invariably a few areas of the form will be found that are over-generous for their requirements; or a few word contractions can be introduced which will provide space to ensure reasonable minimum margins. It should be remembered that we are dealing with 'functional documents', and so if a choice is absolutely necessary then the decision should be on the side of function rather than on, say, grammatical or aesthetic preference.

If further evidence is required that these minimum margins are reasonable, it should be pointed out all forms with marginal holes simply must allow this space—and there are as many continuous forms produced as any other type of form.

Unless there is an unusual circumstance, such as guide marks for folding or for imprinting equipment, to justify printing close to the edge of a sheet, then this practice can be regarded simply as poor workmanship. Bad margins offend the eye and reduce the value of a correctly balanced design.

Before getting around to a detailed and accurate draft of the headings and type matter which will have to appear on a new form, no doubt some quite rough sketches will have to be made to outline ideas of how the form should eventually appear. Particular attention should be paid to part-to-part changes. There will usually be fewer problems, however, if it is only alterations that are being made to an already existing form.

It is always advisable to produce a drafted or re-drafted lay-out for each individual part of the set. If one or more parts in the set are exactly the same except for minor alterations, it is sufficient to show the change, then simply outline the area which is common, and mark this 'BALANCE—SAME AS PART 1', as shown in the order-acknowledgement-delivery form in Illustration 22.

The important point is to ensure that each part of the set is treated and identified as a separate section to be carefully examined on its own for all details.

It is strongly recommended that this procedure should be carried out as described, regardless of whether the form has been newly devised, is an alteration from an existing form, or is an exact repeat of an existing set.

Do not permit the submission of an old sample set, with instructions simply to repeat exactly as the sample.

This type of action tends to discourage any search for improvement in the form. It furthermore encourages the rather risky assumption that simply because a set has been manufactured and used before it must therefore be correct, efficient and suitable for the procedure.

Experience will quickly show the fallacy of such dangerous assumptions, and will bear out how essential it is to clarify completely each detail of the form's design and construction each time it is manufactured.

Illustration 22. Part-to-part changes

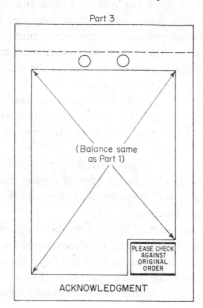
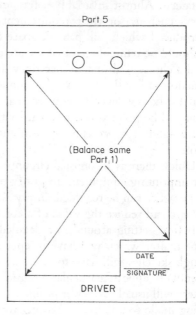

Procedure Write-up

To complete the manufacturing instructions it is advisable and desirable that a brief, but detailed, account should be written-up on the handling of the form from its introduction into the system until its final stages. Particular attention should be paid to how the manufactured form is written or processed, and stating the make and model of any machine used. The treatment of special features such as double stubs or duplicating master parts should be clearly explained, in order that the manufacturers will have every chance to produce the set to the highest degree of functional efficiency.

Drafting Pads

Where a lot of forms designing is contemplated it is suggested that graph sheets, in pad form, and in an overall size of, say, 17 × 13 in (425 × 325 mm) would be of particular advantage in general forms work. Larger sheets may be required for many computer forms. However, this can be simply achieved by using two sheets from the pad, trimming the margin from one sheet to overlap the other, then taping them together in correct alignment. The sheets should be very faintly ruled in pale tints of blue, green, or grey in order that the ruling will not intrude into the actual design of the form. Some people prefer a semi-translucent paper with a 'mirror' or negative image, and in this case the design is drawn on the opposite side of the sheet, using the show-through ruling as guide-lines.

Standard spacing would be in tenths of inches (2·54 mm) horizontally across the 17 in (425 mm) way, and in sixths of inches (4·23 mm) vertically down the 13 in (325 mm) way of the sheet. This would cover the standard $\frac{1}{10}$ in (2·54 mm) character spacing for pica typewriters, accounting machines, and computer-output printers. Be particularly careful, however, with tabulators, as some of these machines have a character pitch (or width) of $\frac{5}{32}$ in (4 mm), although the $\frac{1}{6}$ in (4·23 mm) measurement would cover the standard vertical throw (or line-space) of most machines. Some little difficulty may be experienced if the machine is set to print out at eight lines per inch (3·175 mm depth), although four lines per inch (6·35 mm depth) is coped with on these drafting sheets by allowing one-and-a-half spaces in depth per print-out line.

Naturally, if the machines are of Continental European make, then, of course, their appropriate standard measurements would require to be substituted. If there is any doubt about measurements of pitch and throw of a machine, then samples of the print-out of the machine should be obtained which will allow for both digit and line counts to be made. This would particularly apply to machines which have a variable pitch, or 'set', for their alphabetical characters.

The layout of business forms is primarily a matter of simple drafting, and these ruled sheets allow precise indications of where type matter and rules, etc., should appear. By using such graph paper for drafting, not only will the actual drawing be facilitated, but it will also show immediately if a print-out line or character is being scheduled for an unprintable position. This is vital information at this stage because corrective action can still be easily taken.

It must be assumed here that the requirements for ease of documentation have been taken into account when roughing out this present design. All that really remains now is to measure out carefully the spaces for the columns which will adequately contain the information ultimately destined to be written on to the form. Allowance will also be made for the requisite, or average, number of writing lines.

Type Rules: With regard to type rules themselves, it is best not to allow too great a mixture, and it is quite sufficient to work with three weights only: heavy (equivalent to 2 points), medium, and light—along with a moderately fine dotted, or slotted, rule. Other weights may probably be introduced for display effect, but will not be required for columnar rules. See Illustration 23.

Here again, no inflexible pattern can be laid down to be slavishly followed. A pleasing use of the three weights would be obtained if the top and bottom horizontal rules, with perhaps one heading separation rule, were in heavy weight, with all other horizontal rules in light weight. Vertical rules would be in medium weight, except for any cash columns which would be in a dotted rule. See Illustration 23(*a*).

While being careful not to offend the eye by overdoing the use of different

Illustration 23. Various weights of type-rules

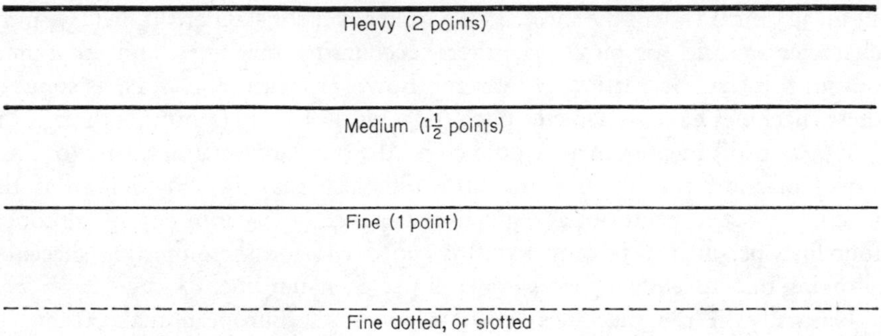

Heavy (2 points)

Medium (1½ points)

Fine (1 point)

- - - - - - - - - - - - - - - - - -

Fine dotted, or slotted

Illustration 23(a). Suggested use of various weights.

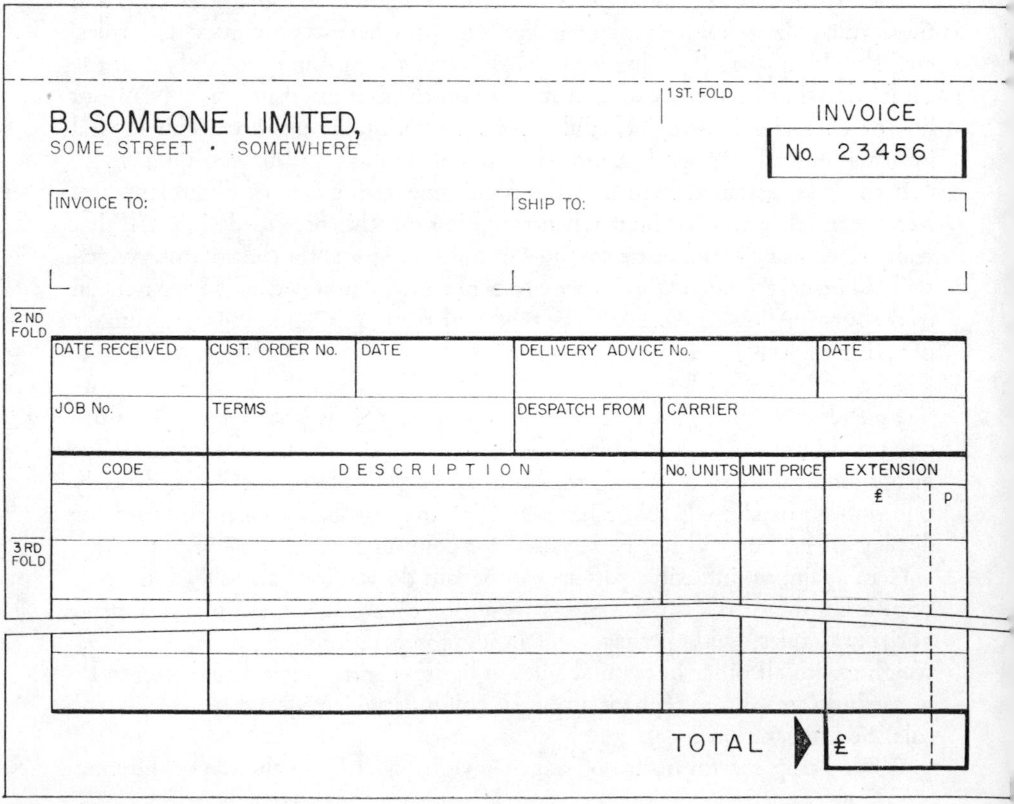

	1ST. FOLD		

B. SOMEONE LIMITED,
SOME STREET · SOMEWHERE

INVOICE

No. 23456

INVOICE TO: SHIP TO:

2 ND FOLD

DATE RECEIVED	CUST. ORDER No.	DATE	DELIVERY ADVICE No.		DATE
JOB No.	TERMS		DESPATCH FROM	CARRIER	

CODE	DESCRIPTION		No. UNITS	UNIT PRICE	EXTENSION	
					£	p

3 RD FOLD

TOTAL ▶ £

weights of type rules, logical separation into sections can be easily highlighted by this means. It can also serve to enhance the appearance of a form, by relieving the otherwise monotone features of a forms layout.

Fold Marks: It may also be noted that fold marks have been indicated. Such handling aids can be introduced with very rewarding performance results for very little extra effort. It is only a matter of keeping in mind such points when the overall handling of the various parts of the sets is being discussed. If the output volume of such a form is fairly high but sporadic, so that folding and stuffing into window envelopes is necessarily done manually, then the inclusion of fold marks into the design could simplify and expedite this operation. The functional ability of the form could thereby be increased at virtually no extra cost.

Positioning: With regard to the actual positioning of each box or column it must be assumed that consideration will have been given to the three basic functions of documentation, storage, and retrieval. In addition, the relationship with other associated documents and the requirements for 'writing' processes must also be taken into account before committing a forms design to paper.

Naturally, handwritten forms present the least critical specifications of all with regard to actual layout, because of the flexibility of the human hand. Nevertheless, some care should at least be taken to permit data to be recorded in an orderly sequence, thus ensuring that wasteful effort and movement will be kept to a minimum. Little effort is required for the human hand to move from the bottom left to the top right of a form. If, however, wasteful actions have to be repeated perhaps fifty or one hundred times per day then it will be realized that some confusion may be created. Such confusion could, in turn, generate unnecessary mistakes.

A horizontal movement from left to right is the natural direction for not only mechanical writing processes but also for handwriting. As far as possible the various entries should be made on a horizontal plane, rather than requiring to be made in a vertical direction. This would be the first thought when trying to decide the sequence of locations to contain particular information—providing, of course, no special priority of information is demanded by associated documents. See Illustrations 24 and 24(*a*).

Similar thinking would apply to typewriter forms, but there would be added complications compared to handwritten forms because of the lower degree of flexibility of the machine. However, every effort should be made to take full advantage of tab stops and other devices designed to increase efficiency and speed documentation on any mechanical writing equipment.

In the following examples it should be noted that in the 'preferred' design, although the size of the form has been reduced, the number of tab stops has

Writing Direction

Illustration 24 —   Illustration 24(a) —

Vertical movement—Undesirable   Horizontal direction—Preferred

                                                                    ENGINE
MAKE_____   MAKE   MODEL   NUMBER

MODEL_____   _____ _____ _____

ENGINE NUMBER_____

been reduced from about thirteen to five. There is little doubt that few typists would bother to set up thirteen stops, but they would surely set up and use five tab stops. See Illustrations 25 and 25(a).

Illustration 25. Trade-in record—Old design.
         (Size $6\frac{1}{4}$" x $4\frac{1}{4}$")

THE WYANZED TRADE-IN MACHINERY CO.

TRADE-IN RECORD

TRADE-IN ON   TRADE-IN ON
NEW MACHINE SOLD £_____   USED MACHINE SOLD £_____

DESCRIPTION_____

_____

PURCHASED FROM_____AT_____

INVOICE No._____DATE_____£_____

WORK ORDER No._____£_____£_____

SOLD TO_____

INVOICE No._____DATE_____£_____

ACTUAL SALE PRICE £_____   SUGGESTED SALE PRICE £_____

SOLD ON BLOCK No._____   MINIMUM SALE PRICE £_____

Illustration 25 (a). Trade-in record—Preferred design.
(New size. $6\frac{1}{4}"$ x $3\frac{1}{2}"$)

TRADE-IN MACHINE RECORD

TRADE-IN ON NEW MACH. SOLD FOR	TRADE-IN ON USED MACH. SOLD FOR	No. 2345
£	£	

DESCRIPTION		
	,	

PURCHASED FROM	AT	PRICE £

DATE	INVOICE No.	PURCH. ON BLOCK No.	W. O. No.	£

SOLD TO		W. O. No.	£

INVOICE No.	DATE	SOLD ON BLOCK No.

MINIMUM SALE PRICE £	RECOMMENDED SALE PRICE £	ACTUAL SALE PRICE £

THE WYANZED TRADE-IN MACHINERY CO.

Another advantage that has been achieved by this form design should be noted for further use. By keeping the headings of each box to the extreme left and above the actual writing line, maximum space for the information has been obtained without losing good appearance.

In fact, it may be agreed that the form is generally smarter in appearance by being ruled into boxes. It is also correctly spaced horizontally for typewriter characters, and spaced vertically for exact double-line spacing.

Spacing: Many otherwise acceptable forms fail, at least partially, in their function because of lack of attention to both horizontal and vertical spacing. Much of this inattention springs from lack of knowledge of the requirements and capabilities of the writing instrument, whether it is a typewriter, teleprinter or accounting machine. Some study must be done on the equipment to be used in order to tailor the form to take fullest advantage of the action of the machine.

Efficiency in Movement: Constant data, as far as possible, should be grouped at the left-hand side of the form, and those entries which are only made infrequently should be kept to the right-hand side of the form.

By this means, in a typewriter or teleprinter operation, there will be no need for the operator on every line to move right across the form from one side to

G

Illustration 26. Typewriter Form — Unsatisfactory.

SOLD TO:					SHIP TO:				

CUSTOMER No.		CUSTOMER ORDER No.			SALES ORDER No.		INVOICE No.		

SHIPPED FROM			SHIPPED VIA		AT			DATE	

PRODUCT	CODE	QTY.	UNIT PRICE	EXTENSION £ P	PRODUCT	CODE	QTY.	UNIT PRICE	EXTENSION £ P
PEAS — SMALL					ONION SOUP				
PEAS — LARGE					PEA SOUP				
BEANS — BROAD					MUSHROOM SOUP				
BEANS — BUTTER					DRIED PEAS				
BEANS — BAKED					DRIED LENTILS				
CARROTS — WHOLE					NOODLES				
ASPARAGUS TIPS					SPAGHETTI				

72 CHARACTERS

the other, but only on those occasional lines which require such entries. In many instances the operator will need to travel only half the width of the form before returning to the first writing position on the next line.

As thousands of lines per day may be entered on particular forms, it will be readily appreciated that a great saving in time can thus be effected by so increasing the functional ability of the form.

This attention to economy of horizontal movement is even more important in the case of a teleprinter application since time here is a very costly factor, and where 'skipping' takes the same time as normal key-stroke spacing.

Although obviously not applicable to tabulator or computer-output printers which take exactly the same time to print each line regardless of size, it is frequently more economical in typewriter or teleprinter applications to incur an occasional few extra writing lines, rather than to involve the machine in an extra 15- or 20-character horizontal movement on every single line. Illustrations 26 and 26(a).

Illustration 26 (a). Typewriter Form — Preferred.

PRODUCT	CODE	QTY.	UNIT PRICE	EXTENSION £ | p	CODE	QTY.	UNIT PRICE	EXTENSION £ | p	PRODUCT
PEAS — SMALL									ONION SOUP
PEAS — LARGE									PEA SOUP
BEANS — BROAD									MUSHROOM SOUP
BEANS — BUTTER									DRIED PEAS

SOLD TO •

•

SHIP TO •

•

DATE •

CUSTOMER NUMBER

CUSTOMER ORDER No.　DATE

SALES ORDER NUMBER

DATE　INVOICE No.　DATE

FROM

SHIP VIA　AT

← 48 CHARACTERS →

From simple enquiries it can be found what is the width of each character, the maximum width of form, tab stop facilities, etc. Vertically, it can be established if the machine has the capability of printing-out six lines per inch as well as three, four, and perhaps eight lines per inch. Line-finding or skipping capabilities whether mechanical or electric, should also be noted.

With this information, the exact location of each typing line can be accurately indicated. Similarly, the location of each character in each line or box may be accurately pinpointed. If word and line counts of the probable data to be recorded have been conducted, there is no reason why, in the normal process of events, data will not fall exactly into the correct position.

Forms which are produced without such basic preparation do not deserve the term 'business-like form', and the manufacturers of such forms can hardly be recognized as forms specialists. For this reason it is important that all people who either use, order, or originate business forms must know the basics of what constitutes an efficient form.

Single or Multiple-Line Spacing: At all times ease of 'writing' will be kept in mind. Always try to design on perhaps a constant single-space or a constant double-space basis, rather than that which requires varying vertical line-shifts of one, two, and even three lines on the same form. Naturally, if the writing machine can be set to skip a constant space it is a great deal simpler to type on than would be a form which requires to be advanced a different number of lines on every vertical shift. Information retrieval would be simplified too, because the location of specific data will be easier to find on an evenly spaced form. Finally, the appearance of the form will be greatly enhanced by regularity of spacing.

Allowance of Space: Once the full width of the type area has been decided upon, it now remains to agree to the sequence of entries to be made horizontally. The items which have a fixed number of digits will be added up with, if possible, one space added to each side of each item to allow for separation between these items. The balance of the space in the line can be split among any other variable-digit items in accordance with their probable requirements. Do not allow, say, 18 spaces for a date entry when 10 spaces may suffice—except when endeavouring to reduce to a minimum the number of tab stops. Allow any extra space to the variable-digit items.

As far as possible, try to allow one clear space on either side of a vertical rule. If this is not possible, then a single clear space may have to be split by the type rule—although this is advisable only on sprocket-fed forms because their exact position in the machine will remain constant on each successive form after the initial setting.

It happens frequently in computer forms that a rule must fall exactly between two characters or digits and great care must be taken in production. In these circumstances make sure that the type-rule, if not hairline, is of a fine weight. If the form is not sprocket-fed, or the output-printer can emit its own numerical punctuation, then it may even be sufficient to indicate the position of item separations by means of only partial dividing rules. See Illustration 27.

It is because of this need for great care in precisely locating exact print-out

Illustration 27. Partial dividing rules

QUANTITY	CODE	DESCRIPTION	PRICE PER UNIT	AMOUNT £ p

positions that the use of graph-type paper for all layouts has been recommended. By this means there need be no chance of confusion about the exact location of vertical rules and line positions. In addition, the position must also be indicated with precise measurements written on the working copy.

Equal care must also be paid to horizontal ruling. One of the most common failings lies in not allowing sufficient space between horizontal rulings for the print-out line while allowing far too much space for the headings. See Illustrations 28 and 28(a).

Illustration 28. Undesirable spacing. (Drawn on graph paper)

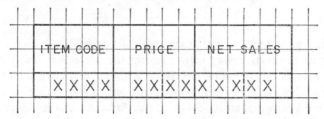

Illustration 28 (a). Preferred spacing. (Drawn on graph paper)

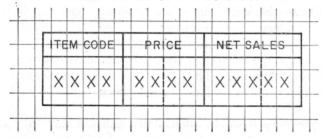

It must be agreed that the 'preferred' Illustration 28(a) not only looks better when printed-out, but obviously makes a much simpler job of setting up the form on the machine for correct print-out position.

The layout in Illustration 28, which is *not* recommended, very often indicates the wrong mental approach to business forms. It would seem that this has been looked at and approved as an unprocessed piece of print with little or no regard for its eventual ability, as a functional document.

At all times, in an efficient business form, it is the data which is being recorded that is important—not the headings. Therefore, the data should be highlighted as far as possible—and the best way to do this typographically is to ensure that there is reasonable white space left around the information. As far as possible avoid cramping the areas allowed for print-out.

Type for Headings: Similarly, the type which is used for headings should be neither large nor obtrusive, and should be kept uniform throughout the headings on the form. If there are any lengthy passages of text matter on the form, it is advisable to set these in a different type than that used for the headings. If not a different type-face, then at least a different size is recommended.

Bold or distinctive type styles are not desirable for headings on forms and these type-styles should be kept for display purposes or for high-lighting a particular item only. The object of the layout of a business form should be to make the recording of information, and its eventual retrieval, as simple and easy as possible while maintaining a pleasing overall typographical balance.

Highlighting

Highlighting, to focus attention on particular areas of a business form, is a simple but most effective way of improving the functional ability of a form. Furthermore, this can frequently be done without increasing the cost of production of a form at all, or by increasing cost only a very little.

Again a correct mental attitude is desirable. An active and inquisitive approach to the overall problems facing a forms application, and a thorough knowledge of all details of the system are the bases for such an attitude—to which should be added some reasonable knowledge of the possibilities which might be available to produce the requisite improvements.

There is really no substitute for imagination and ingenuity, but knowledge of what advantages can be taken of certain circumstances or processes will help to stimulate original thought. The following simple examples may help those who have not previously thought along these lines.

Type and Type Rules: It will be assumed that sufficient knowledge of printing types has been acquired to take full advantage of italics and of light, medium, bold and ultra-bold weights of types, as well as a range of type rules for columnar and display purposes.

Coloured Ink: If a form has been ordered in two ink colours, then full advantage should be taken of this to highlight areas of the form which would benefit from easy and quick identification. Since one is already committed to the cost of a second colour, then here is a circumstance which can be utilized to increase efficiency or effectiveness without substantially increasing cost.

Again, only a thorough knowledge of the application can decide which areas would benefit from special emphasis. Common sense should dictate the maximum number of areas which should be thus treated for the greatest benefit. Too many highlighted areas, by confusing the eye, will quickly nullify any advantage.

For the purpose of illustration, let it be assumed that the 'Total Amount' area of a form is of paramount importance. This figure not only advises the customer of the amount owing, but in this circumstance it also must be transferred to various other statistical documents. Several thousand forms per day are thus processed, and so it is important that the figure should be prominently displayed and be readily accessible.

It will also be assumed that, in the original design, the area allowed for this important item will have left ample clear space surrounding the maximum possible digits in order that the figures may stand out clearly.

If a decision is made to print the form in two colours, say black with a dash of red in the heading area, then an opportunity now arises to make further use of the red secondary colour without becoming involved in any heavy extra cost.

The simplest effect would now be to print in red the type rules which surround the 'Total Amount' area. If this action is decided upon it should be remembered that a type rule printed in red, as opposed to a black or similar dark ink, will lose 'strength' and 'weight'. Therefore, to retain these features, always increase the thickness of a type rule if printed in red or a shade obviously lighter than a strong colour. Furthermore, if fine rules are used there may be insufficient 'body' even to allow proper recognition of the weaker ink colour.

It is usual to allow 50 per cent to 100 per cent increase in weight of rules if they are to be printed in a lighter secondary colour than the base ink. This means that, generally speaking, type rules of $1\frac{1}{2}$ points or 2 points could be increased to about 3 points and 4 points. It is scarcely worth the effort of printing in a light secondary colour type rules of less than 2 points, because the colour will hardly be discernible to the casual eye. The primary object of emphasizing the area will thus have been defeated. The desired effect will have at least been considerably reduced.

Make sure, therefore, that type rules in such circumstances are of sufficient weight to allow the ink colour to perform its intended function of highlighting. Maximum effect should always be the target.

Use of Type 'Sorts': If it is found to be insufficient simply to print in colour the type rules around the particular area requiring attention, there are innumerable other variations and techniques which will help to increase to the desired degree the impact of highlighting. For example, in addition to the rules the words 'Total Amount', plus perhaps a bold arrow, or some such solid type-piece, could also be printed in the secondary colour to encourage the eye to travel to the desired area. See Illustration 29.

Alternatively, as above but with a further variation along similar lines. See Illustration 29(*a*).

Shading and Tinting: Probably the most effective way of highlighting specific

Illustration 29. Highlighting—Use of sorts (1)

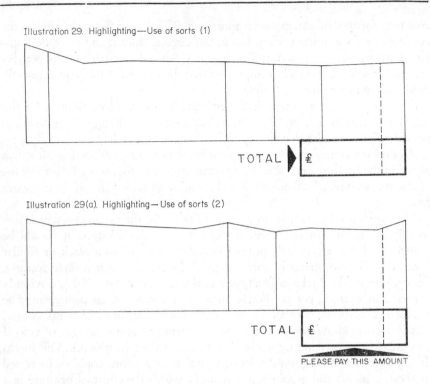

Illustration 29(a). Highlighting—Use of sorts (2)

sections of forms or documents is by means of tinted areas, which can be produced by most printing processes. Tinting is probably the most versatile method of focusing attention to specific areas. Many different effects can be devised to achieve this end. Unusual shapes can help the effect, and often cost little extra.

The decision on whether or not to use a tint may be governed by cost. Cost, in turn, is dependent upon the printing processes available, quantity required, and quality desired or needed. Only by a considered look at these factors, together with a reasoned appreciation of the potential advantages of the tint in relation to the functional ability of the form, can a proper decision be made with regard to the true evaluation of 'cost' in any situation.

Generally speaking, fine quality tints can be produced by the lithographic process, which lends itself with great facility to this feature. However, particularly with the development of plastic and rubber letterpress printing plates, all but the very finest screen printing can be very adequately produced by the other printing processes as far as forms requirements are concerned.

In a printing process, whether relief (letterpress), planographic (lithography), or intaglio (gravure, engraving), a tint of a colour is simply an optical effect created by printing with a stipple pattern. To the human eye the weight of the colour of the ink has apparently been reduced. The degree of colour which will be discernible is controlled by the density of the stipple or screen. This density is usually referred to as a 'screen percentage'; that is, a tint of 75 per cent screen or 40 per cent screen.

This means, of course, that on a business form a contrast can not only be achieved by using two distinct colours, but a further distinction can be obtained by using tints of differing colour density.

Another feature which makes this device very effective is that a tint can be produced in almost any shape to aid the visual impact.

Strip-shading or Tinting

Probably the most common modern use for a tint in a business form is as shaded horizontal bars or strips, common to most stock listing forms. These tinted strips or bars have a very functional purpose indeed. Much of computer or tabulator output comprises line after line of statistical data printed horizontally across the face of the form, which may be up to 16 in or 18 in (400 or 450 mm) wide. Reading the data can therefore impose a considerable strain on the eye when trying to follow each line across the full width. The tinted horizontal strips are printed on as a visual aid to help the eye from straying from the particular line of information which is being read.

Tinted strips may also be introduced into specially designed forms for similar purposes. Further variations can be utilized to make distinctions to particular parts of the horizontal tint. A few examples of possibilities of such combinations are illustrated overleaf. Illustrations 30, 30(a), 30(b), and 30(c).

As will be realized from these variations of shading, there are many possibilities for combinations of tints which can be used for the purpose of highlighting —thus increasing the functional ability of a form. Such possibilities must always be kept in mind at the design stage.

Dual-Purpose Forms: By the intelligent and thoughtful use of strip-tinting it is often possible to extend the function of a document, as in the form in Illustration 31.

It can frequently be found that within a company one form design could cover the requirements of two, or more, separate departments. In the illustration used, the company had two distinct spare-parts departments whose records were required to be kept entirely separate. Instead of two different forms, it was found to be much more economical to devise one form and order twice the quantity. There is the further advantage of not having to check on supplies of two different forms at two locations, and also in reducing the total number of different types of forms in use. The tendency to accumulate unconsciously an overabundance of different forms can easily become a real headache in a large organization.

Illustration 30. Shaded column headings and codes.

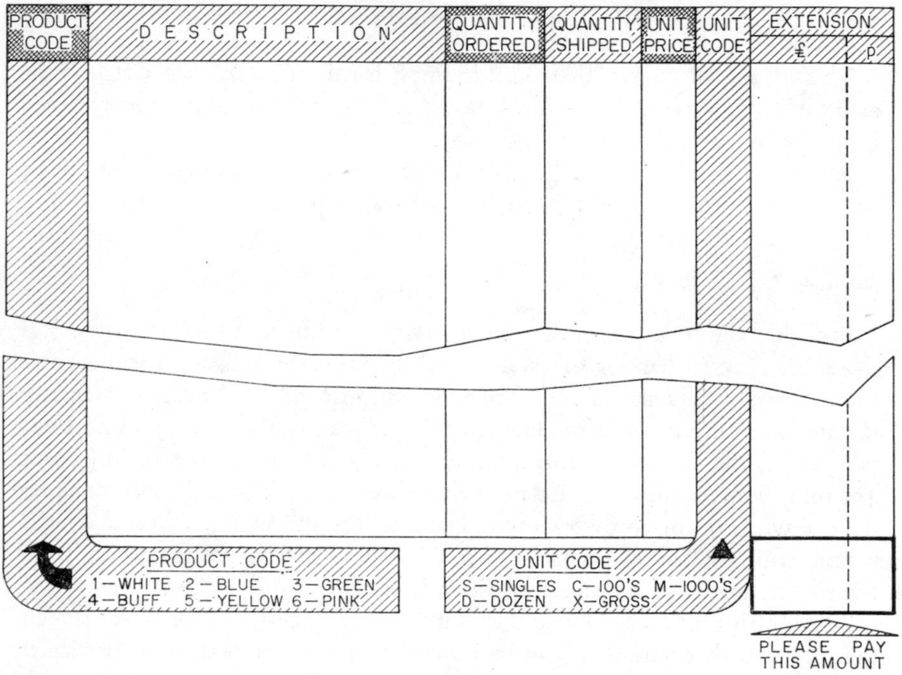

PRODUCT CODE	D E S C R I P T I O N	QUANTITY ORDERED	QUANTITY SHIPPED	UNIT PRICE	UNIT CODE	EXTENSION	
						£	p

PRODUCT CODE
1—WHITE 2—BLUE   3—GREEN
4—BUFF 5—YELLOW 6—PINK

UNIT CODE
S—SINGLES C—100'S M—1000'S
D—DOZEN   X—GROSS

PLEASE   PAY
THIS AMOUNT

Illustration 30(a). Bar shading.

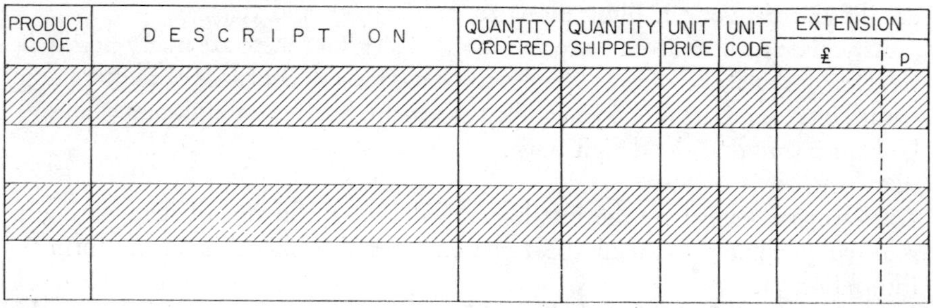

PRODUCT CODE	D E S C R I P T I O N	QUANTITY ORDERED	QUANTITY SHIPPED	UNIT PRICE	UNIT CODE	EXTENSION	
						£	p

Illustration 30(b). Two weights of shading.

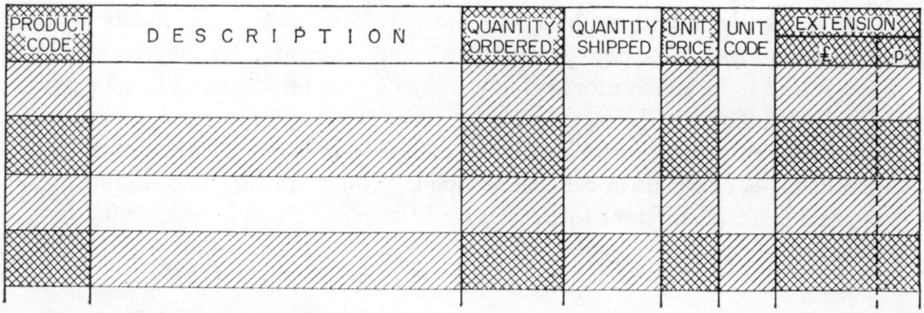

PRODUCT CODE	D E S C R I P T I O N	QUANTITY ORDERED	QUANTITY SHIPPED	UNIT PRICE	UNIT CODE	EXTENSION	
						£	p

Illustration 30(c). Broken-bar shading.

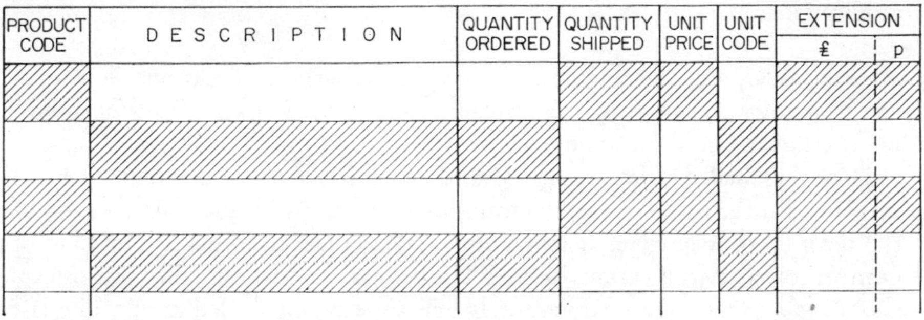

PRODUCT CODE	D E S C R I P T I O N	QUANTITY ORDERED	QUANTITY SHIPPED	UNIT PRICE	UNIT CODE	EXTENSION £	p

Illustration 31. Dual-purpose Form.

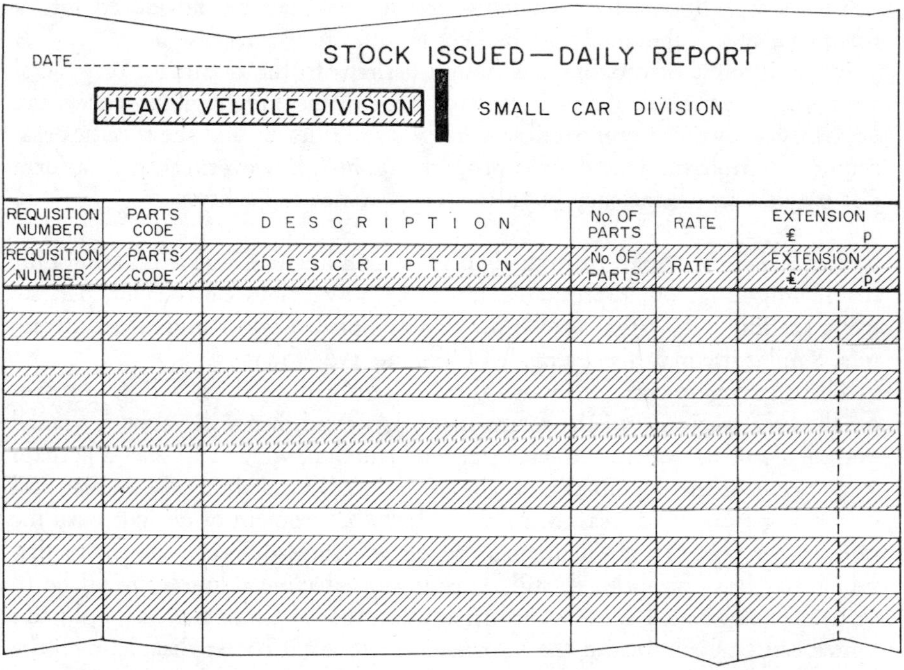

STOCK ISSUED—DAILY REPORT

DATE_____

HEAVY VEHICLE DIVISION   SMALL CAR DIVISION

REQUISITION NUMBER	PARTS CODE	D E S C R I P T I O N	No. OF PARTS	RATE	EXTENSION £ p
REQUISITION NUMBER	PARTS CODE	D E S C R I P T I O N	No. OF PARTS	RATE	EXTENSION £ p

The above form was designed so that the tinted strips were two print-lines apart. The Heavy Vehicle Division used the shaded lines, and the entries were therefore double-spaced. Similarly, the Small Car Division used the clear lines. By this means there was little chance of any confusion in recording the items against the correct division's Spares Department.

Naturally, further similar uses could be discovered; for instance, in companies who require to keep separate payroll systems. In fact, when carefully thought out, this treatment can be found to apply with advantage to many applications.

Assisting Analyses: The function of providing efficient analyses within a form can be greatly enhanced by using shading correctly. An example of this might be as follows. See Illustration 32.

Here the shaded areas are not spaced regularly, but are intended to focus attention on the totals of each commodity in each classification. At the foot of the form there is an effective and simple arrangement to facilitate a number of comparisons between various figures. The total sales to date and the same figures shown as a percentage of these totals will appear in a shaded area, while last year's figures to this date and this year's quota to this date will appear in an unshaded area to permit ease of comparison.

Such simple means by which higher efficiency can be introduced into a form or a system should always be kept in mind for forms design.

In the interest of economy, although perhaps to the detriment of general appearance, it must be pointed out that many of these highlighting effects can be achieved by using comparatively heavy type rules around the specific areas requiring emphasis. Tinted areas properly applied, however, can give a form not only an air of efficiency but also an appearance of quality.

Shaded Characters: Apart from the benefits which might accrue from using tints for highlighting, other profitable functional advantages can be obtained by using shading—this time, shaded (or tinted) alphabetical or numerical characters. Similar use may also be made of 'outline' type founts.

There are many occasions when there is information which will be constant on the great majority of the forms being processed, but will vary on a small percentage of the forms. If the constant information, which appears on perhaps 75 per cent of the documents, can be pre-printed, then obviously a great deal of writing time can be saved. Nevertheless, the problem of dealing with the odd 25 per cent of the documents, which will have different data from that which has been pre-printed, still remains. An effective solution would be to print the pre-printed constant information in shaded characters of a light tint which can be easily read if the information applies. If not applicable, then the new variable information can be typed over the faint shaded characters, or outline characters, thereby simultaneously nullifying the original instructions while substituting new directions. Again, some new trains of thought may be stimulated by the following example. See Illustration 33.

The foregoing examples are only a few of the many types of circumstances where considerable benefit may result from the judicious use of shading for accentuating or highlighting areas of a form for specific purposes. It is now

Illustration 32. Design to assist analysis.

SOMEONE CANNED FOOD COMPANY

PROGRESSIVE SALES REPORT AND ANALYSIS

WEEK ENDING_____

PRODUCT	TOTAL SALES	NEW SALES	RE-ORDER SALES	LOSSES		NEW ACTS.	No. OF SALES
				PREV.NEW	RE-ORDER		
SOUPS:							
TOMATO							
GREEN PEA							
LENTIL							
SCOTCH BROTH							
MINESTRONE							
TOTAL SOUPS							
MEATS:							
WHOLE CHICKEN							
CHOPPED HAM							
TOTAL MEAT							
JAMS:							
STRAWBERRY							
PLUM							
APRICOT							
TOTAL JAM							
TOTAL TO DATE							
PER CENT TO DATE							
LAST YEAR TO DATE							
QUOTA TO DATE							

Illustration 33. Outline and shaded characters.

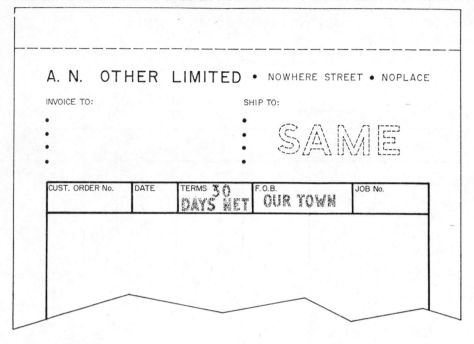

only a matter of keeping such ideas in mind when finally considering the possibility of expanding the functional capacity of a form within the overall system or application.

Distinguishing Parts of a Set

Coloured Parts: The most popular and the most effective way of distinguishing the various parts of a business set is to print each part on a different colour of tinted paper stock. By this means it is virtually impossible that a part can get into the wrong file, or even get into the wrong pile of copies for filing, without being noticed immediately.

The colours most commonly available would be white, blue, yellow, buff, goldenrod, green, and pink. There may also be a few specials—such as salmon. Various paper mills offer varying colour combinations. Not all of these colours, however, will necessarily be available in all weights and grades of paper, so check this point out before becoming too involved in other matters.

It is also still usual to designate a title to each part of the set to indicate its ultimate purpose.

Designations: The use of designations on business forms is very common and serves many useful purposes. Not only do designations give a distinguishable title to identify and thus help to control each part of the set, but they may also indicate the distribution of the part once it is separated from the rest of the set.

This can be important, as the particular part may contain certain information which is pertinent to only one specific department. Conversely, the part in question may for special reasons have certain information suppressed by means of block-outs, cut-outs, or desensitized areas.

In other circumstances it may be advantageous not only to know the ultimate destination of one part, but it may also be important that all, or some, departments receiving one copy of the set should be aware of the distribution of the other parts of the set. In this case the list of distribution of all parts could be printed in the designation area.

Since the primary purpose of a designation title is to identify, it should therefore be set in a bold-face type. At least it should be in a type-face which will quickly distinguish the designation from the body matter of the form.

Ideally, designations should appear in another ink colour from that used for the body matter. This can be simply done in those cases where the consecutive numbering is printed in a contrasting colour, such as red, and where there are facilities for printing the designation simultaneously. However, since cost may be a decisive factor, a second colour may not always be permissible. If a secondary colour is not available, then reasonable efforts should be employed to obtain emphasis for the designations by other means, such as in size and style of type employed and the location of the designation on the sheet, etc.

Designations can be made more prominent by ensuring that there is plenty of clear white space surrounding them. This is one reason why, if possible, they should be located in close proximity to a deep, clear margin, with reasonable space separating the designations from the text matter.

Location of Designations: The location of designations may be dictated by the availability of spare space, but it is advisable that where possible the designations should appear in the same location on each part of the set. This may not always be possible as, for example, when combining a formalized multiple-part Bill of Lading or waybill with a company's invoice/acknowledgement form. Generally speaking, however, one location for all designations is more efficient.

The proposed method of filing the parts would be an important factor in deciding the location of designations, particularly in sets which use one colour of paper stock for all parts. The designations must be in a location which will permit ease of access in order to identify the part by means of the designation. The location may be decided upon in relation to the manner in which the document will be filed, either in open files, in post binders, or in other filing systems. See Illustrations 34 and 34(*a*).

Illustration 34. Inefficient designation locations.

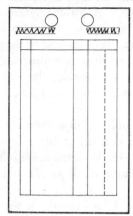
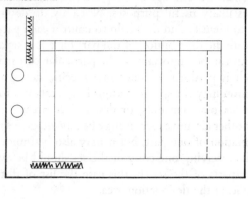

Illustration 34(a). Preferred designation locations.

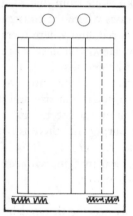
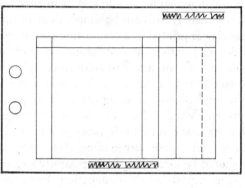

Efforts should be made to make designations as brief as possible and to avoid ambiguity. For example, avoid using terms such as 'Office Copy'—unless it is used to indicate that this is the duplicate part of a two-part section (i.e. original and 'copy') of the set which is to be directed to the office. It is much safer to state briefly the department or the function to which the part applies, e.g. 'Invoice', 'Acknowledgement', 'Stores', 'Control', 'Dispatch', etc.

Changing designations from part to part can be costly. Not only must the press be stopped to permit the change to be made, but the various parts must now be carefully kept separate and in a particular sequence. This latter requirement is not too difficult if all the parts are of a different colour of paper stock. However, if only one colour of stock is used, then it is absolutely imperative that each part must be carefully watched or transpositions of parts within a set can easily occur—with perhaps adverse results.

With these circumstances in mind, and because of the potential saving in manufacturing costs, it should always be remembered that it may be possible to print a list of the distribution of all parts on some, or all, sheets comprising the set. This could perhaps be printed on the stub of a glued set, or in small type at the foot of the form as in the example following. See Illustration 35.

Illustration 35. Distribution shown on all parts.

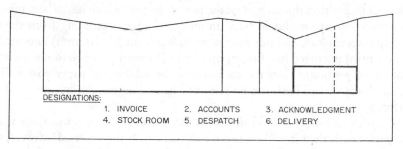

DESIGNATIONS:
1. INVOICE	2. ACCOUNTS	3. ACKNOWLEDGMENT
4. STOCK ROOM	5. DESPATCH	6. DELIVERY

Sequence of Parts

Various points should be kept in mind when deciding the sequence of parts in a set—particularly a glued-stub set. These points should cover not only priority of parts with regard to clarity of impression, but also the sequence in which the parts will be removed from the set. This should be considered as it will have a bearing on the final construction.

Naturally, the first parts of the set will have sharper impressions while the latter parts of a set will usually become progressively less clear. Those departments or functions which require a high degree of legibility will therefore be positioned near the front of the set in some order of priority.

If, however, one or more parts of the set—such as an acknowledgement— must be detached before a carbon-interleaved glued set is entirely separated, it is important to ensure that such parts are 'inside' copies. This is advisable because if the top or bottom part of a set is detached then, either way, a carbon will be exposed and liable to cause smudging or may be damaged in subsequent handling operations. Whereas, if the part is located in an inside position, then when the part is removed the form will remain virtually unchanged as far as further handling is concerned.

Unless there is a specific reason for doing so there is usually no real need to remove the carbon, even though its associated paper part has been detached. If it remains inside the set it will not interfere with any further handling or processing of the set. There is, therefore, no necessity to complicate the

H

construction or manufacture of the set unnecessarily by introducing any un-required perforations.

Extended Carbons: If, for some reason, it is felt that both part and carbon should be removed then this is most easily effected by using an extended carbon paper. This type of carbon was described in Section 2 for use in identifying the location for separating a set into two sections.

The carbon would require to be at least $\frac{1}{4}$ in (6 mm) longer than the rest of the set and perforated in the stub position in a similar manner to the paper parts. It is usual to position this carbon on the face of the part which has to be removed. The extended carbon should have an uncoated edge protruding from the set, to keep fingers clean, and this may be anything from $\frac{5}{8}$ in (16 mm) uncoated to $\frac{7}{8}$ in (22 mm) uncoated (i.e. fingergrip of $\frac{5}{8}$ in (16 mm) plus $\frac{1}{4}$ in (6 mm) for the protruding portion). Thus the carbon and the subsequent paper part will be quickly located, and both can be removed in one movement by means of the perforations.

Since this carbon is an odd size from the rest of the carbons in the set, and also perforated, then it will be more expensive than the others. However, this extra expense could easily be compensated for by the advantage of the speed and convenience of locating and removing the part and carbon simultaneously. See Illustration 36.

Illustration 36. Extended carbons.

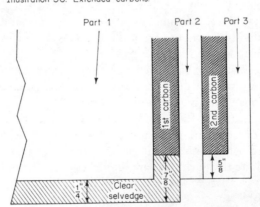

Consecutive or Sequential Numbering

The decision to employ consecutive numbering is usually governed by the necessity to implement a strict control over a forms application. Naturally, cost and necessity will influence the decision to number forms. However, many advantages can be obtained through consecutive numbering, for example, by a tighter security control of cheques, invoices or purchase order forms. Consecutive numbering will also provide accurate and quick means of assessing forms usage at any time, thus reducing the possibility of running out of forms at a crucial moment.

This frequent, and unnecessary, source of trouble arises from the delay in reordering supplies of forms, because nobody has been able to check quickly on usage and stock on hand. Then follows panic re-ordering, with the resultant tendency to errors. Just as regrettable is the unfortunate fact that there is now no time to assess the efficiency of the form, nor time to consider or implement proposed changes in the form.

For whatever reason consecutive numbering has been decided upon, make sure that the actual number is positioned so that it may fulfil its function. On a form which is liable to be filled with figures it is essential that this number should be prominently displayed in order that the particular form may be identified quickly and accurately.

Displaying Sequential Numbering

As in other cases where emphatic presentation is necessary, a little imagination will pay dividends. Again the object should be to focus attention on the number, and also to facilitate recognition.

Regrettably, many forms designs give the impression that the consecutive number was a pure afterthought. It appears to have been positioned in a very haphazard manner in any available open space. The ultimate result is a rather apologetic and self-conscious impression that the number has somehow intruded into, but is no part of, the design.

It is a great mistake not to start the design with the consecutive number as an integral part of the basic plan. Many methods of displaying the number to the best advantage can be found, and the examples in Illustration 37 may help to suggest other variations.

Again, location on the form is of vital importance and must be decided upon in relation to the method of filing proposed. This consideration is frequently overlooked, and as a result much inconvenience may be unnecessarily caused.

In the case of an ordinary open-top filing cabinet it should be fairly apparent that the number should appear on the uppermost section of the form. This would mean that a form could be easily identified by a quick riffle through the file, without necessarily removing the document from the file, as would be necessary if the number appeared on the bottom half of the form.

The exact location may probably be governed by the nature of the information and data which the form contains. Nevertheless, the position of the sequential number must be one of the basic considerations in the design of a business form. It should not be, nor should it appear to be, included on the form as an afterthought. It must be part of the whole layout of the form. It is an important item, so ensure that it gets proper prominence.

File-Hole Punching

A feature which would have a strong bearing on the location of a consecutive number would be file-hole punching for post or ring binders. In the circumstances where this type of filing is involved, every effort should be made to position the consecutive number at or adjacent to the opposite side from the file holes. This is necessary in order that the number will be in the most advantageous position for ease of reference when the part is secure in the binder. See Illustration 37.

Similar care would require to be taken if filing is done by means of clips or clamps, although, of course, there is a choice of which edge should be secured with this method of filing.

Aperture Cutting

A device which can be incorporated into a design to increase the functional capacity of a form is an aperture cut. This is a cut-out on a form which will provide a similar function to that of the aperture in a window envelope. Not all forms-manufacturing machines have the facilities which will provide aperture cutting and, as a result, the process may be expensive. However, only the *total* cost of the *whole* operation can indicate whether the additional cost is prohibitive or acceptable. Again, the value of increased efficiency will usually be the decisive factor in considering such a device.

A careful feasibility study would be absolutely essential before embarking on a project such as this. In some circumstances, however, valuable benefits and efficiencies could result from such a forms application—if properly planned.

Functional requirements will always influence the adoption of a particular form construction or design. In this instance, an aperture cut will allow for the display of, say, computer-printed names and addresses on tear-off, pre-paid, reply cards. This could be part of a folded document, with perhaps personal information concerning rates, taxes, dividends, questionnaires, etc.

Likely circumstances which might call for an aperture-cut form would most commonly arise where it is desirable to send a notice of some kind, requiring the minimum possible effort to the recipient of such a document in order to ensure or at least encourage a reply. This might be used in a postal advertising or sales campaign; or perhaps by a local government body seeking statistical information.

Illustration 37. Numbering related to open file.

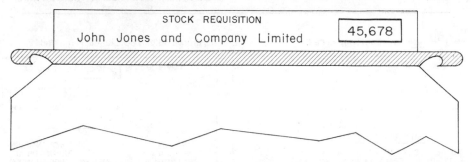

STOCK REQUISITION
John Jones and Company Limited
45,678

Illustration 37 (a). Numbering — head file holes

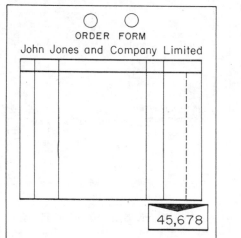

ORDER FORM
John Jones and Company Limited

45,678

Illustration 37(b). Numbering — foot file holes

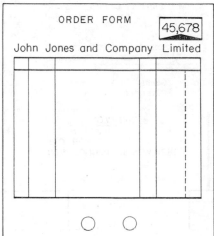

ORDER FORM
John Jones and Company Limited

45,678

Illustration 37 (c). Numbering — side file holes

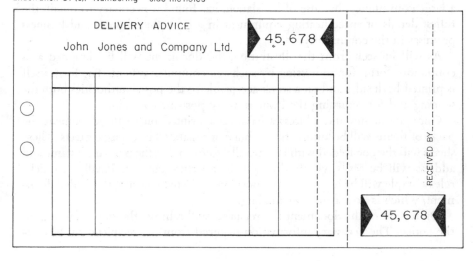

DELIVERY ADVICE
John Jones and Company Ltd.
45,678

RECEIVED BY

45,678

Illustration 38. Aperture-Cut Form. Side 1.   Illustration 38(a). Aperture-Cut Form. Side 2.

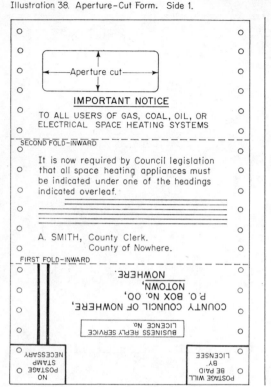

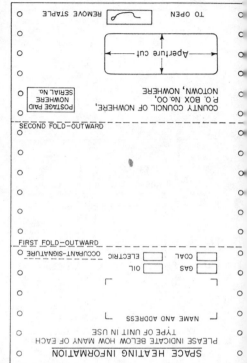

Procedure For Aperture-Cut Forms: The illustration presents the case in which a large community, because of legislation, has found it necessary to obtain the fullest details of space-heating equipment in all dwelling houses and business premises in the community.

As will be seen from the illustration, the document will be designed as a continuous form, for addressing by such as a computer system. The form itself is printed both sides and on a stock acceptable to the postal authorities both for sending and for returning the business reply post-card section.

Once the names and addresses have been printed on to the document the packs of forms will be automatically burst or separated into single sheets. These sheets will then be folded with two parallel folds so that the recipient's name and address will be easily visible through the aperture cut-out. Finally, a quick-release staple will be inserted in the position indicated securing the folded document, which is now ready for mailing.

On receipt of the document the recipient will remove the staple and unfold the notice. The necessary information required from the recipient can be con-

Illustration 38 (b). Card when folded.

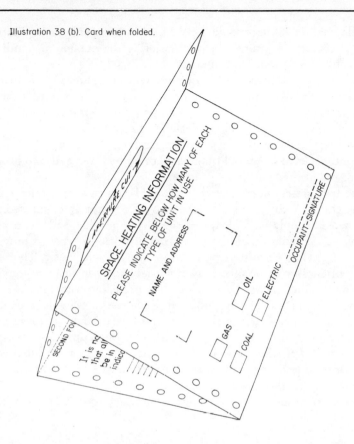

veniently entered in the information spaces allocated on the reverse side of the notice. That portion can now be detached, by means of the tear-off perforation, and it is now ready to be returned in the post without any further processing by the recipient.

There would be three basic objectives with such a form construction:

(a) By providing a simple and minimum-effort document, encouragement would be given for the maximum number of replies;

(b) By manufacturing as a continuous form, addressing could be done expeditiously on a computer output-printer or similar equipment;

(c) By providing, where various postal rates exist, for both dispatch and return on cheapest possible service rate, and thus taking fullest advantage of any possible economies in transmission without involving the recipient in any expense whatever.

Particularly with regard to the last two items, it will be quickly seen that considerable financial savings could be obtained in large-volume applications; although, of course, the prime object of ensuring the maximum number of replies will still be of paramount importance.

In the case of (b) the forms can be addressed on a computer system, or other mechanical writing equipment, from information which will probably be readily available from memory storage. To attempt to do this operation by the conventional means of typing single documents could involve a sizeable and costly typing pool for this specific job. Furthermore, the stuffing of the folded document into its envelope would be complicated by having also to handle a return-paid, pre-printed envelope.

With the aperture-cut document there would be no envelope stuffing at all. In fact, the cost of two sets of envelopes would be entirely eliminated. The document would simply be folded, mechanically if possible, and secured by a single staple. This staple should be of the unclasped loop type, to provide a secure fastening while ensuring ease of removal by the recipient. The whole procedure will be seen to be much easier and less costly in many aspects than the more conventional method described in the preceding paragraph.

Similarly, in item (c), depending on local postal rates applicable, it could be that considerable savings in postal costs may be effected by requiring only printed-matter rates outgoing and post-card rates on return, as opposed to charges on letter rates where envelopes are used. When items in hundreds of thousands, or even greater volumes, are involved, then savings in postage per unit are certainly worth close consideration.

For unusual circumstances this is an application which warrants remembering.

Information-Suppression

The situation frequently arises where it is desirable that information which appears on some parts of a multiple-part set should be eliminated from one or more of the other parts. It may, therefore, be of interest to look at some of the more common methods of information-suppression. Some of these methods have been touched on in the pages dealing with striped, patched, or cut-out carbons in Section 2, so these should also be considered.

Again the handling procedure and writing method must play a part in deciding the most suitable method to be adopted. These considerations may be purely practical, such as the limitations which might be incurred in handling procedures, difficulty in the forms manufacturing process, or even from a forms cost point of view.

Another important point, however, must be kept in mind. That is, to what degree of effectiveness must the information-suppression be kept. Is it enough simply to reduce the possibility of being able to read the information easily, or is it vital that the information must on no account be conveyed by that particular part of the form?

For example, on a receiver's copy of a delivery advice it is sometimes felt advisable to suppress the column containing quantity, or number of items or cartons, to encourage a physical check being made on incoming goods. In this case, a block-out pattern may be over-printed on the required area, thus making difficult any reading in that area, as subsequent information would be virtually obliterated to the casual eye. However, the characters imprinted on the paper by a typewriter can sometimes be deciphered—and, therefore, for situations in which security is essential it will be realized that the block-out method is not entirely successful. The fact of overprinting with a form of block-out surely advertises that information in this area is being suppressed. The curious will thus be invited to investigate.

There is another method which is simple and obvious, though frequently overlooked. If the sheet concerned with information-suppression is, or can be made, Part 1, then it is a simple matter to substitute in the typewriter a black/white typewriter ribbon for the more usual black/red ribbon. Thus, to suppress information on the top copy of, say, a contract or an insurance document, simply type on the white top sheet with the white portion of the ribbon.

While this method may be quite acceptable in many cases, it does call for considerable extra concentration by the typist to ensure that the change is correctly made from the black portion of the ribbon to white and then back again before resuming the other typing on the form. Careful design can reduce inconvenience to a minimum, by perhaps ensuring that all information to be suppressed is kept to one location—and, if possible to one line. The introduction of adequate markers indicating when to change from black to white and then back again can help to reduce errors at this point.

The ideal solution to the problem of information-suppression would be to ensure that the portion of the part containing the unwanted information cannot get into wrong hands at all.

Staggered Perforations: This latter suggestion can frequently be implemented by staggering the stub perforations in a glued-stub set. The following diagram will show the re-location of the perforation on Part 2, the customer's part. This now means that after the set has been typed up in the usual way and pulled apart, the portion of the part containing the unwanted information remains on the stub and is discarded with the stub and interleaved carbons. Therefore, the elimination of the information is done automatically, and it is not left to chance that somebody will remember to remove the unwanted portion of the part.

This method cannot be implemented efficiently on sets without a stub. See Illustration 39.

Note also in this illustration that Part 2, the customer's part, could be made

Illustration 39. Staggered stub perforations.

STOCK PRICE	DISCOUNT CODE	UNIT PRICE	QUANTITY	DESCRIPTION	AMOUNT £ p

A. N. OTHER LIMITED | STOCK ORDER   PART 4 ORDER FILE

A. N. OTHER LIMITED | STOCK ORDER   PART 3 STOCK ROOM

STOCK PRICE	DISCOUNT CODE	UNIT PRICE	QUANTITY	DESCRIPTION	AMOUNT £ p

A. N. OTHER LIMITED | STOCK ORDER   PART 2 CUSTOMER

STOCK PRICE	DISCOUNT CODE	UNIT PRICE	QUANTITY	DESCRIPTION	AMOUNT £ p

A. N. OTHER LIMITED | STOCK ORDER   PART 1 ACCOUNTS

STOCK PRICE	DISCOUNT CODE	UNIT PRICE	QUANTITY	DESCRIPTION	AMOUNT £ p

slightly larger than the other parts, so that it could be easily located and torn out while the balance of the set remained intact as a unit, if circumstances called for such a procedure.

Presenting Copy

The ultimate step before the actual manufacture of the forms is the presentation of final copy for production. The clarification of every last detail can, and should, be agreed upon at the draft or layout stage. To demand a succession of printer's proofs of the finished article is an out-of-date custom—and is generally wasteful, time-consuming, and unnecessary.

If specific art-work is required for a 'cut' or 'block', then, of course, a proof is usually submitted. Original artistic design could be difficult to imagine for visual impact, and there is justification for proofs here. Similarly, if the heading, for one reason or another, is complex then a proof of that portion of the form may also be justified.

For the main body of the form, however, type styles and sizes and type-rule weights can be decided upon at the layout stages, and indicated on the final pencil copy. The positioning of columnar rules and headings should not be considered as a matter of aesthetic 'feeling' or 'taste'. This is a functional document, so headings and type-rules must be in precise and exact locations—and this is best not left to chance, but should be indicated by explicit measurements which must be strictly adhered to. The printer must follow these fixed written measurements. If the layout is properly drawn and marked, then there is no excuse for any errors in the forms which are finally produced.

It must be fully appreciated that it is unrealistic to expect production departments to resolve correctly any areas of ambiguity. This can only be done by those who were responsible for the development and design of the form. It should, therefore, be understood that if any points of doubt exist then the copy should be returned by the production departments to the originators of the form for clarification. It should now be obvious how important it is to have the instructions on the final copy as clear and complete as possible. Doubt can only cause delay.

Printer's proofs should be regarded as a courtesy service for final approval only, not as another stage in the design of the form, nor as a last opportunity for re-designing. Furthermore, proofs cannot be produced under actual running conditions and, therefore, can only be an approximation to the finished job. This could encourage misleading assumptions with regard to columnar spacing, for instance. On the other hand, there should be no room for uncertainty if clear instructions are given.

It is for the above reasons that mention has been made of the value of graph-type ruled sheets being used when designing business forms. This is equally important both for mechanically 'written' forms and for hand-written forms.

With both horizontal and vertical rulings to indicate normal movement units, it is a simple matter to draw columnar rules in precisely the location desired. With the addition of written measurements there should be no possibility of dubiety in the minds of production personnel.

If measurements and instructions are shown with a coloured pencil, they will then be more conspicuous and will not be confused with the design itself. See Illustration 40 (p. 112).

See Illustration 40 (p. 112).

FINAL SUMMATION

It is not considered, of course, that the last word has been written on this subject. Indeed, this text can only be a general appreciative look at some of the more or less common aspects, and many specific areas could be gone into in much greater detail.

If the reader, however, has now obtained a conscious awareness of some probable areas of improvement, of possible methods of form construction, or

Illustration 40. Presenting copy.

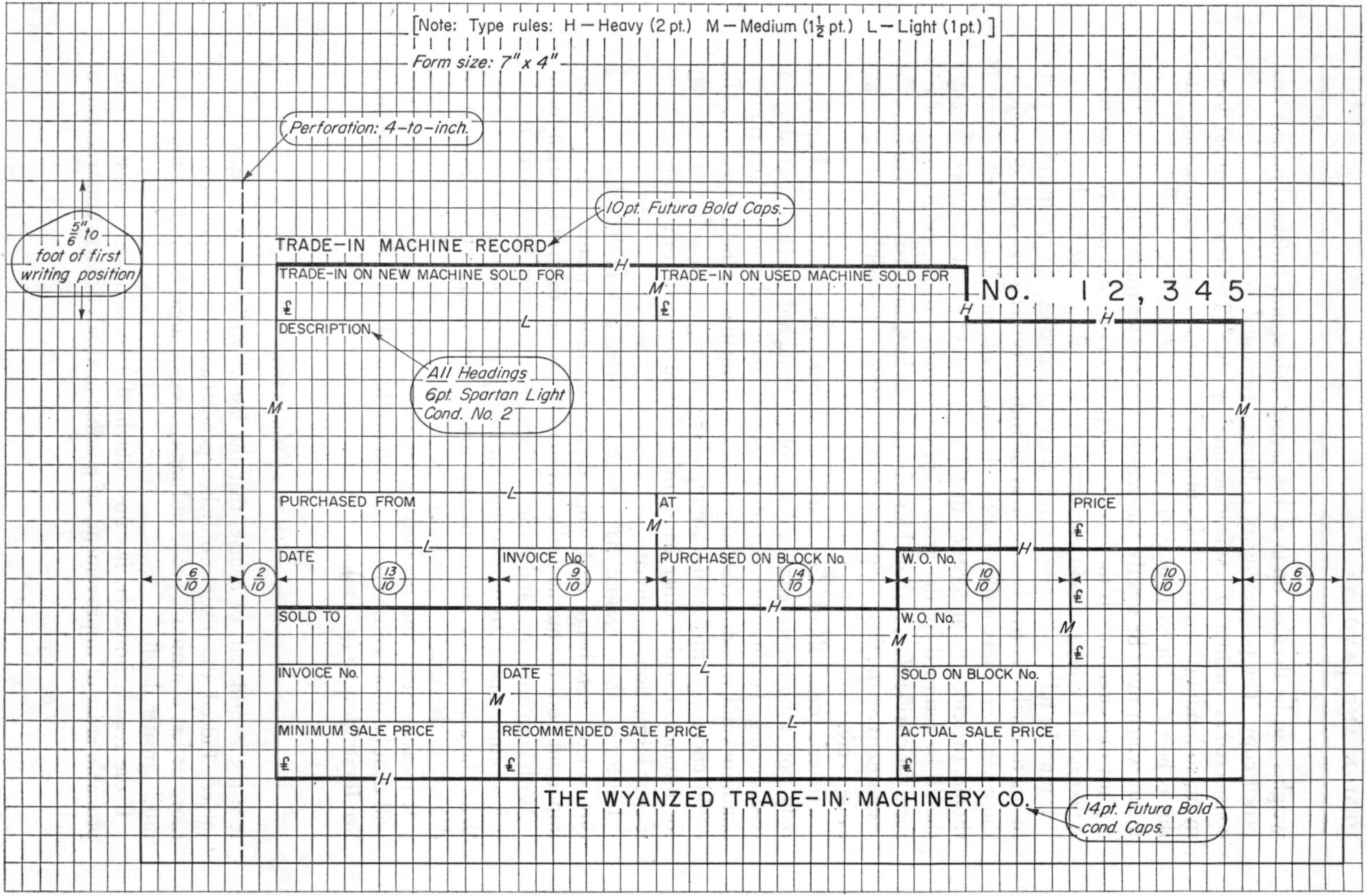

[Note: Type rules: H — Heavy (2 pt.)   M — Medium (1½ pt.)   L — Light (1 pt.)]

Form size: 7" x 4"

Perforation: 4-to-inch.

⅚ to 1
foot of first
writing position

TRADE-IN MACHINE RECORD

10pt. Futura Bold Caps.

All Headings
6pt. Spartan Light
Cond. No. 2

No. 1 2 , 3 4 5

14pt. Futura Bold
cond. Caps.

TRADE-IN ON NEW MACHINE SOLD FOR

TRADE-IN ON USED MACHINE SOLD FOR

DESCRIPTION

PURCHASED FROM

DATE

INVOICE No.

AT

PURCHASED ON BLOCK No.

W.O. No.

W.O. No.

PRICE

SOLD ON BLOCK No.

ACTUAL SALE PRICE

SOLD TO

INVOICE No.

DATE

MINIMUM SALE PRICE

RECOMMENDED SALE PRICE

THE WYANZED TRADE-IN MACHINERY CO.

of the correct basic concepts of form design, then much has been achieved. But very little will be accomplished without the further addition of the 'magic ingredient', common sense—which manifests itself best in an intelligent atmosphere of tolerance and encouragement. It is certainly unrealistic to assume that one group of people have a monopoly on common sense, which is why tactful questioning of all people involved is recommended during a survey.

Not only should it be realized that the information and techniques discussed herein can now be utilized when the appropriate situation arises, but it should also be realized that non-traditional or unorthodox methods can often be developed to implement an unusual requirement. If the need is great enough, then, usually, given a reasonable time to consider the problem, an effective solution can be developed.

The most dangerous situation by far, however, is that wherein inefficiencies exist unsuspected and uncontrolled. It is for this reason that a correct, watchful attitude should be cultivated. This is not to say that everything that is being done is necessarily wrong, but rather that all applications may be suspect and should, therefore, be questioned at regular intervals.

Finally, it is sincerely hoped that through the reading of this text some measures will be instituted which may help to reduce those mountains of wasted time, which still fail to be recognized as such, simply because they do not pile up in great heaps on the floors of offices throughout the world.

There is a lot to be done!

INDEX